FENG SHUI PURE & SIMPLE

Written By: Bridget Baker
Edited By: Andrea Baker

Text copyrighted © 2017 by Bridget Baker

All rights reserved

No part of this book may be reproduced, or stored in a retrieval system, or transmitted in any form, or by any means, electronic, mechanical, photocopying, recording or otherwise, without express written permission of the publisher.

ISBN 9781521282526

Cover Photograph by Bridget Baker
Copy Edited by Andrea Baker

DEDICATION

For my mother

She not only gave me life, but instilled me with a love of books.

When she gave me that, she gave me the world.

TABLE OF CONTENTS

INTRODUCTION TO FENG SHUI — 1
Chi; The Breath of Life — 2
Yin and Yang Concepts — 9
The 5 Transformations — 17

INTRODUCTION TO THE BAGUA — 29
Wealth/Prosperity — 37
Fame/Reputation — 40
Relationships — 42
Family/Growth — 45
Health — 47
Children/Creativity — 50
Knowledge — 53
Career — 55
Helpful People — 58

BUYING OR SELLING A HOUSE — 61

FENG SHUI CURES AND REMEDIES — 99

SPACE CLEARING — 106

HOME BLESSING CEREMONY — 113

CONCLUDING THOUGHTS — 117

INTRODUCTION TO FENG SHUI

The literal translation of Feng Shui is Wind and Water. These are two of the strongest forces in nature, yet neither ever has to strive or strain to reach their goals. Wind and water represent the forces of the natural world that we can't live without. Feng Shui had its beginnings in rural China where people relied on fishing and agriculture to make a living. The fishermen knew that without wind to fill their sails they could not get their boats into good fishing waters or get them back home. Too much wind would tear up their sails and destroy their boats. The farmers knew that not enough water would mean a drought that destroyed their crops; but too much water (like a flood) could also destroy their crops and wash away the topsoil that grew the crops that sustained their families. What they needed was moderation and balance, and this is what we get with Feng Shui.

The universe shows us what perfect balance is. We are surrounded by it. We have oceans with just enough salt to keep the water from becoming infested with bacteria, but not so much salt that marine life can't flourish. We have an atmosphere with enough oxygen so that we can use fire; but not so much oxygen that fire gets out of control. This is what Feng Shui is all about – Balance and Harmony. Feng Shui is not superstition, philosophy or religion. It is the art and science of living in harmony with the environment. Good Feng Shui is nourishing Chi, a balance of Yin and Yang and a productive link between the Elements. Once you understand those three building blocks you know everything you need to know in order to attract health, wealth and happiness in your personal life, as well as fame and recognition in your professional life.

CHI; THE BREATH OF LIFE

Many practitioners like to describe Feng Shui as the Chinese art of placement, and I am one of them. This four-word description is an excellent summation of this ancient art that can bring us health, wealth, happiness and peace through the creation of harmonious environments. Although this book concentrates on creating harmony in the home, Feng Shui applies to every layer of the environment, from the cosmos down to the inner self. We are all affected by the total impact of all layers of the environment, but as you would expect, the layers of the environment that are closest to us have the greatest impact. For example; when it is very cold outside you will be affected less by those extreme temperatures when you are inside a house or shelter, because that layer of the environment is closer to you. If there are two of you within the shelter and one has warm mittens, that person will be less affected by the cold because of the additional layer separating them from the cold temperature.

The beginnings of Feng Shui go back far before recorded history. In Asian cultures, the myths and legends surrounding this ancient art were handed down through oral tradition and we have no way of verifying their accuracy. The literal accuracy of these stories is not important, you should think of them simply as a means of teaching and preserving the concepts of Feng Shui. Legend has it that Fu Hsi; one of the early rulers of China saw a tortoise emerging from the River Lo as the waters were subsiding after a series of devastating floods. On the back of this turtle was a pattern of dots that were clustered in separate areas of the shell. Fu Hsi recognized the order of the Universe in the dots when they were converted into numbers. The number of dots in each cluster will add up to 15 no matter which way you look at them – horizontally, vertically or diagonally. Because of this, the pattern of numbers is sometimes referred to as the Magic Square. It is the arrangement and sequence of these numbers that later evolved into what we refer to as the Bagua in Feng Shui. You will also sometimes see the alternate spelling of Pa'-Kua or you may hear it referred to as the Lo Shu Square. In the following graphic you will see this Magic Square depicted in a grid pattern where you can easily see how the numbers are laid out. This figure is often used in the west when studying Feng Shui because it is so easy to follow. When this grid is laid over a room, or a house, or a land formation, it forms a map showing where every aspect of life is anchored energetically.

BAGUA GRID

4	9	2
3	5	7
8	1	6

In the upcoming section on the Bagua, you will learn which life aspects correspond to which numbers, and where you can find them in your own living environment.

Unlike the maps you are probably accustomed to; the Bagua and this grid are oriented with South at the top. In China, the sun and warm winds that brought good fortune to the farmers came from the south. The sea that brought good fortune to the fishermen was also located south of the country. Bitter cold winds and violent winter storms came from the north as well as the hot, searing dust storms of summer. For these reasons, the early Chinese considered south the direction from which good fortune arrived, and north was a direction from which one required protection. When using the Bagua map, it should be oriented so that south is at the top. The south section in the grid shown above is the one that contains the number nine.

The underlying philosophy behind Feng Shui is the understanding that the universe and everything in it is made up of energy. Scientists in the field of quantum physics are only now beginning to understand what Feng Shui enthusiasts have been practicing for over 4,000 years. We know today that the atom is *not* the smallest particle of matter, and when you start working on the subatomic level; all things are made up of the same substance. The only difference between say a horse and a 3-carat diamond is the number and arrangement of waves and particles. Quantum physics is a fascinating subject well beyond the scope of this book, but if you delve into it further you will see that when the ancients said, "Where your attention goes, energy flows" they were centuries before their time. Even without understanding quantum physics, you can use this information to make changes in your life using the art of Feng Shui. However, if you want a scientific explanation for *why* it works, you may want to do some reading on the subject of quantum physics.

MOVEMENT OF CHI

Chi is the word we use in Feng Shui when we are talking about energy. Whether you call it energy, Chi, Ki, Orenda, Qi, Prana, the Life Force or the Cosmic Breath, it is all the same thing. If you will think of Chi as Cosmic Breath, it will help you understand the way Chi travels through your space. The first steps you will take when applying Feng Shui to a space involve the movement of Chi.

RUSHING CHI

It is Chi, or energy, that is the life force that supports all of us and you need to make sure that there is an adequate amount of new energy flowing into your space. You also need to make sure that it is lingering there long enough to nourish you through your home. If the Chi is rushing through our space too quickly, it does not stay long enough to nourish us – similar to what happens with some eating disorders or when you have your stomach stapled. The food comes in, but it is not there long enough for our bodies to benefit from the nutrients. Rushing Chi can be a challenge if your house is too close to an overactive source of Chi like a major highway or thoroughfare. It can also be caused by long, unbroken hallways or a floor plan where there is an exit point (like a door or window) directly across from the source of Chi and nothing in the path to slow it down. If the Chi is rushing through your personal space, it creates a chaotic atmosphere that is the opposite of the peace and tranquility we want to achieve with good Feng Shui practices.

Think about the way designers lay out a drugstore. While the primary purpose of a drugstore is to fill prescriptions, the big profits are made on the other sundries that you might buy there. If a customer were able to come right in the front door and step up to the pharmacy counter, that would probably the only purchase that that customer made. Remember, the customer and his money is the life force that supports and nourishes the store and the owners. Designers purposely lay out the store so that a customer has to weave through sales displays for batteries, hairspray, greeting cards and candy bars in order to reach the pharmacy and pick up a prescription. The customer has to run the same obstacle course of sunscreen, baby toys, pain relievers and magazines to get back to their car. The designers know that somewhere during that journey you are bound to see something you forgot you needed (or never knew you wanted) and will end up buying more than you originally intended to. These impulse purchases will provide more nourishment to the drugstore owner in the way of additional profits.

By arranging your living environment according to the principles of Feng Shui, you can cause the Chi that enters your home to meander through every nook and cranny, lingering in your space to provide more nourishment and support. If the Chi is rushing too quickly, you can slow it down by putting obstacles like furniture or room dividers in its natural path to divert it into other rooms or areas that it is passing by. You can slow it down by lining its path with plants, artwork or other distractions that will give it pause. Chi will also travel faster over smooth surfaces, so see if you can think of a way to use area rugs, drapes or soft furnishings to reduce its speed.

MAINTAINING THE FLOW

Like any guest who hopes to be invited back, Chi needs to know when it is time to leave. If the tempo or speed of the Chi moving through your home is too slow, it will become stagnant. This can happen when there is no way for the Chi to exit (for example having no back door) or when the natural exit path is blocked by furniture, shutters or decorative objects in your home. When it moves too slowly it becomes what we call stagnant Chi. If you are surrounded by it, you will stagnate too. This often happens in corners, alcoves or niches because Chi will always follow the easiest route. Chi follows roads and waterways (This is why you find thriving cities built along these formations) and it will follow the traffic patterns in your house. You need to draw it into places like corners by attracting it with light, movement or beauty. Chi will also slow down or stagnate if it encounters low level energy – the kind of energy that you get from grime or clutter. Or from people with low level energy; sick people, complainers or depressed people all can lower the quality of energy in your home and you need to learn how to counteract that.

Let's use moving water to demonstrate how energy moves through a house. If you were to watch a gently flowing stream at a spot where it widens into a shallow pool, you would see one of two things. For our first example, the shallow pool is clear and sweet, because the water from the pool is drained further downstream after it lingers in the pool a short while. However, in a second situation, the "back door" to this shallow pool has been dammed up, or perhaps it has been clogged with small branches blown down by a storm. The water has nowhere to go, so it stays in the pool and eventually becomes stagnant and murky. Because it is no longer moving, the water may become filled with algae and provide a breeding ground for mosquitoes and bacteria. There are three things that you need to do in order to maintain clear, sweet water in a little pool like this. You need fresh water flowing in, you must provide the right conditions to make it linger, and you need to provide a way for it to exit. This is exactly what you need to do with the vital energy, or Chi, that flows through your home.

THE MOUTH OF CHI

The front door is the primary place where the Chi enters your home. Make sure that the entrance is large enough to allow in ample amounts of Chi, and check to be sure that the door is in good working order. If stiff hinges or a warped frame make the door hard to open this will inhibit the free flow of Chi. Anything that makes it hard for *you* to come in the front door also makes it difficult for Chi to enter. Some of these difficulties might actually originate outside the house. You want to be sure that the steps or pathway that lead up to your front door are clean, clear of obstructions and in good repair. You also should make sure that the entrance is well lit and that the house numbers are large and visible from the street. Check your landscaping too. Overgrown bushes that force you to swerve or duck on your way to the front door will have a detrimental effect on the energy entering your home as well.

It would be easier to know where we need to adjust the flow of Chi if it were visible, but since it is not, try the following exercise that I sometimes use to evaluate the path of Chi in a house.

Imagine yourself standing at the front door to your home and visualize a sweet breeze blowing through the open door. Mentally watch where the breeze goes and ask yourself:

Where does it seem to slow down?

Where is it blocked by furniture or walls?

Does it miss some corners entirely as it moves from the point of entry to the point of exit?

Where does it speed up?

Does it rush directly from the entrance to a back door or large window in direct line with front door?

If you have a floor plan of your home, make a copy and repeat this exercise using an erasable pencil to trace the movement of Chi through your home. Start at the front door and move through the entire space weaving through each room and in and out each window until it reaches the exit. When you have completed your drawing, make note of which places seem to be out of the path of energy in your home. Make note of any obstacles in your home which prevent the smooth flow of Chi and notice where it moves too quickly.

Now sketch in the major pieces of furniture in your home just as you have them arranged now. Retrace the original lines. Do you notice any changes? Are those changes improvements? Perhaps you have already thought of some ways you could improve the flow of Chi in your home by rearranging your furniture. If you have thought of some changes, sketch them and see what happens.

CREATING THE RIGHT ATMOSPHERE

Chi comes from three sources: First we have Celestial Chi which includes weather, seasons and time. Then we have Earthly Chi; either natural, such as landscapes, mountains and magnetic fields or man-made, including buildings, dams, and roadways. And lastly we have Human Chi which can come from thoughts, the energy in your body, or the social forces that flow between people. Certain energy patterns will make it easier to accomplish whatever it is that you want to do. A young couple starting up the career ladder and building a family will thrive in a very different environment than the older couple preparing for retirement.

We also need a variety of specific energy patterns within the larger ones. If you need to concentrate your focus to study for a test, you will require a much different type of energy than you will need when you want to cast off the distractions and pressures of the working day and prepare yourself for sleep. Later in this book, you will be learning many ways of attracting and redirecting Chi to balance the flow of energy in your space. Feng Shui is well known for using mirrors for this purpose, but you can also use color, texture, placement, sound and any number of decorative objects to accomplish this same objective. Once you understand what Chi is, and how it moves, you will intuitively sense when you should make changes and the best way to make them.

YIN AND YANG CONCEPTS

ACHIEVING TRUE BALANCE

The concept of Yin and Yang is most commonly expressed by the graphic shown above. This symbol is called the Taiji or Tai Chi. At the end of all the text I use to explain this concept, you will see the graphic again, and if I have done a good job of explaining things, you will be able to see how the picture symbolizes the entire story.

Sometimes you will hear this concept reduced to the difference between male and female. While this is a fast way to get your mind going in the right direction, it is only a tiny fraction of the concept. Yin and Yang are polarities or to put it another way, Yin and Yang are complementary opposites. In the Eastern concept of spiral time, they are different phases of the same energy. There cannot be one without the other. For example, there is no such thing as cold. Cold is the absence of heat. You cannot experience the energy of cold without having the experience of heat. That is why you see a small dot of white in the black part of the Taiji and a small dot of black in the white part. For every Yang expression of energy is shaded by Yin energy, just as every Yin expression of energy is tinted by Yang energy.

TIME AND SPACE DIMENSIONS

Feng Shui covers both the dimensions of space and time. You can see the effects of the passage of time as you look at the concept of Yin and Yang. Day moves into night and summer will become winter. High noon is extremely Yang and Midnight is extremely Yin. Late morning is a mixture that is more Yang than Yin and late afternoon is a mixture that is more Yin than Yang. The farther away from noon you move, and the closer to midnight you get, the more Yin the energy becomes. Spring is a season where the Yin energy of winter becomes infused with the Yang energy of summer and it will become more and more Yang until we reach the peak of summertime. Once it reaches that peak, it becomes more and more Yin as we move into fall and eventually winter. When the opposite extreme is reached in the passing of time (first example) or the changing of seasons (second example), the cycle begins again.

One of the easiest and most effective ways to understand the difference between Yin energy and Yang is to see the two polarities side by side where you can see the different ways they express their respective energies through the same object, action or event. The lists that follow have pairs of words that hold either Yin or Yang energy. Read each pair and pause before reading the next to absorb the meanings. Continue reading them until you can actually feel the difference between Yin energy and Yang energy. When you finish, see if you can think up your own examples of something Yin cycling through time or space to become Yang.

Chi Thought:

It is the interaction of Yin and Yang that creates change.

The first word in each pair carries more Yin energy and the second one, in bold type, carries more Yang energy. After you read through these words, think of all the areas in between the two that is a mixture of both Yin and Yang energy. For example; between black and white we find many shades of gray and between day and night we have early morning, and late afternoon and evening. Most of the time one or the other will dominate, but other times there is a more even balance.

*Yin-**Yang***

Rain-**Sunshine**
Winter-**Summer**
Earth-**Heaven**
Night-**Day**
Moon-**Sun**
Dark-**Light**
Valley-**Mountains**
Death-**Life**
Damp-**Dry**
Cold-**Hot**
Low-**High**
Shady-**Sunny**
North-**South**
Midnight-**Noon**

Inward-**Outward**
Back-**Front**
Bottom-**Top**
Quiet-**Loud**
Slow-**Fast**
Stillness-**Motion**
Empty-**Crowded**
Contracting-**Expanding**
Inner-**Outer**
Passive-**Active**
Lethargic-**Energetic**
Mother-**Father**
Weakness-**Aggression**
Fatigue-**Vigor**
Sadness-**Joy**
Intuitive-**Rational**
Female-**Male**
Imagination-**Logic**
Creative-**Analytical**
Odd Numbers-**Even Numbers**
Soft-**Hard**
Religion-**Science**
Curved-**Straight**
Sweet-**Salty**
Bland-**Spicy**
Asymmetrical-**Symmetrical**
Black-**White**
Faith-**Reason**
Family-**Self**
Reading-**Wrestling**
Saving-**Spending**
Meditation-**Preaching**
Being-**Doing**
Yoga-**Aerobics**
Philosophy-**Mathematics**
Nature-**Technology**
Listening-**Talking**
Receiving-**Giving**

You can't judge one of these as good or bad; each has its place and function. I'll use restaurants to illustrate. If you take your family to a fast food restaurant you'll notice that it has almost exclusively hard surfaces; tile floors, Formica counter-tops and plastic chairs none of which absorb the sounds of the other diners. The décor and uniforms of the employees are usually bright colors like orange, yellow or red and the service is quick. The predominantly Yang atmosphere of the restaurant makes you feel hurried and energetic with the subtle message that you need to hurry up and rush off to another errand.

If someone takes you to a romantic restaurant you will notice muted colors in the décor, and lots of soft surfaces in the way of carpets, tablecloths and upholstered chairs. The lighting will be dimmer, and instead of the clatter of silverware and trays, you will hear low voices and mood music. This creates a more Yin atmosphere that makes you want to linger and may give you the feeling that you could stay all night. The servers usually wear black and white – the Yin energy of the black makes you feel relaxed and the Yang energy of the white lets you know they are ready to serve you.

Both environments fulfill their function and both restaurants will make a profit. The first one by serving a lot of customers in a short time so the lower priced meals are multiplied by many transactions per day and the second one by serving fewer customers higher priced meals and creating an atmosphere that encourages diners to linger over coffee and dessert resulting in a higher tab per person.

Both Yin and Yang energies also serve a function in your home, which is why you want to have a balance of both. Depending on what room it is, you will probably find that one or the other will tend to dominate, but if it goes too far to either extreme, you can adjust the balance by using the principles of Feng Shui.

Practical Exercise: Do you think you can sense the differences between Yin and Yang now? Try looking around the room you are sitting in and categorizing the objects you see as either Yin or Yang. Most objects will be a mixture of both Yin and Yang. This is good, because those objects have balance. Try your hand at categorizing the people who might be in this room, yes they will be either male or female, but gender aside, you will notice that each person gives off either more Yin energy or more Yang energy. Someone we might describe as a type A personality would qualify as Yang while a person who exhibits more Yin energy might be described as laid-back, or mellow. After you feel comfortable categorizing objects and people, move on to the colors around you, and the time of day, the season, the climactic conditions (inside and out) even the activities going on around you. Developing this ability is what Feng Shui is all about. If you discovered that most of the colors and textures and objects around you were predominately Yang, think about how easy or difficult it is to relax in this room. Now, get a mental picture of the room in your house with more obvious Yin characteristics, is it easier to relax in that room? Then think about what kind of activities you plan for the most Yang room in your house and how you use the most Yin room. Are you trying to sleep in an overly Yang environment? Think about ways you could introduce more Yin energy and make it more conducive to sleeping. Are you attempting to study or conduct business in an area that is overly Yin for those activities? Think of ways you can reduce the Yin energy and add more Yang characteristics. Making those changes to the room will make you much more productive. You probably thought of some obvious changes like increasing the light in your desk area, or using softer colors in your bedroom. As you go through the chapters in this book you will become even more finely attuned to the balance or imbalances in your environment and find some practical ways to improve it.

THE PASSAGE OF TIME

The interaction of Yin and Yang creates change. In Feng Shui, we are constantly working towards the ideal of Yin and Yang that will bring us good fortune. Because the passage of time is continually changing the energy in our environment, we must constantly adjust our personal environment to stay in balance. Feng Shui is not a static science; it is the art of continually adjusting to changes and thus maintaining our balance and harmony with nature. We do this naturally whether or not we have ever heard of Feng Shui. We wear a different type of clothing in the winter than we do in the summer. Not only is it made of warmer materials and styled to expose less of our skin, but we also gravitate towards darker colors as well. When summertime comes, we adjust our wardrobes again, and we will also adjust our diet. We naturally seek out foods that are more Yin (salads over stew for example) to counteract the additional Yang energy of the summer months. If we don't do this, we are bound to encounter misfortune in the way of less vibrant health. We have learned over time that in order to enjoy optimum health and vigor we have to adjust our diet to accommodate the current climate. You have probably been making Feng Shui adjustments to your home as the seasons change without ever thinking about the changes as Feng Shui remedies. In the wintertime, you might start keeping a warm afghan over the back of your sofa because it is a convenient place for it to be when you feel a chill. You might move the chairs in the living room closer together to make conversation easier because in the wintertime you entertain people inside rather than out on the deck. We could go on and on about how people change their wardrobes, diets and living environments to accommodate the seasons, but you probably understand the concept now. Seasonal and climactic changes are not the only influences that cause us to act this way. We make similar changes as we get older, change our family size, or as we change our goals in life.

FITTING IT ALL IN

One of the reasons for learning the principles of Feng Shui is to make you more conscious of the subtle changes that happen around you and to give you some direction as to what kinds of adjustments will balance and harmonize your environment. Not all of the changes are as easy to spot as the passage of time, but you're going to be introduced to some material that will make it easier to notice and adjust for more subtle changes.

Moving from Yang to Yin and back again is simply the nature of life. A baby starts out very Yin – receptive, impressionable and dependent – and as the child grows he or she will exhibit more and more Yang characteristics – such as action and independence – until this reaches a peak at the prime of life. In mid-life it is natural to again begin developing more Yin characteristics; to go inward and explore more spiritual realms. As we age further and retire from the Yang influence of a job, we begin down-sizing our homes and friendships become more important than things. Gradually we exhibit less and less Yang energy until the contracting Yin energy brings us to old age and physical death. We may not like to think about such things in our culture, but this death and decay provides the breeding ground for new life. Everything that a person created during their season of Yang energy provides a foundation for the life that comes in the next cycle. Perhaps this is the monetary endowment you leave for your children or the life skills you passed on or the condition in which you left society and the planet. Actually, this spiral is a much more empowering concept of the passage of time than the linear concept of time that we are accustomed to. Look at the Taiji again as we leave this topic, and notice the large end of the Yang energy in the upper left as it gives way to the black Yin energy which is growing stronger as it moves around the spiral. See this figure as noon moving into sundown, dusk and eventually midnight before it spirals back around to sunrise, midday and noon. Now see the bottom of the figure as the deepest winter with all its energy buried under ice and snow.

As the small tail of summer's Yang energy melts the snow and brings the springtime, it continues to grow in the clockwise spiral until midsummer brings us up to the top of the Taiji where Yang is fullest. Use your own examples of Yin and Yang interacting to come around full circle.

If I've done my job well, you should now be able to understand why looking at the Taiji is a reminder of balance in all things.

THE 5 TRANSFORMATIONS; CREATING HARMONY

In Feng Shui it's not enough to just know that everything is made up of energy. In this section, you are going to learn the characteristics of the different types of energy that make up everything in our universe.

Once you are familiar with these energy patterns, you will learn how they work together to create either harmonious conditions or stressful conditions. You will learn which patterns you want to avoid and how to make corrections when you cannot avoid them. In Oriental philosophy, the 5 Elements of Fire, Water, Wood, Earth and Metal make up the world and every expression of life in it. It is the interaction of these 5 Elements that determines the nature of the energy in motion under a given circumstance and time. When we talk about Wood energy or Fire energy, we do not necessarily mean a plank of wood or an open flame in the literal sense. A burning candle is just one example of Fire energy; a burning lightbulb would be another. Because of their potential, both the lightbulb and the candle hold Fire energy even when they are not burning.

The elemental energies you will learn about here apply to everything in the universe, not just solid objects. Color and sound are prime examples; and even people will have one of the elements as their dominant form of expression. In this section you will learn what the associations are and how to use this information to create harmony in your environment. In order to do that you will need to know the characteristics of each element and how they interact with each other.

First I'll start by describing each of the 5 Elements and their characteristics, and then I will explain the various relationships between the elements and how to use them.

CHARACTERISTICS OF THE 5 ELEMENTS

The energy of the elements can best be understood by reading and absorbing the following summaries which express each element through symbols and associations. Symbols are much richer than words and these symbolic representations will help you feel the different phases of the elements more clearly.

Fire Element

Movement: Outward
Mental System: Action
Climate: Heat
Color: Red
Shape: Triangular or radiant

Earth Element

Movement: Stabilizing
Mental System: Knowing
Climate: Dampness
Color: Yellow, Brown
Shape: Flat or Square

Water Element

Movement: Flowing
Mental System: Will
Climate: Cold
Color: Black
Shape: Irregular

Metal Element

Movement: Hardening
Mental System: Organizing
Climate: Dryness
Color: White
Shape: Round or Oval

Wood Element

Movement: Upward
Mental System: Planning
Climate: Wind
Color: Green
Shape: Vertical or Tall

THE NOURISHING CYCLE

Take a look at how these 5 Elementals interact with one another beginning with the nourishing (or productive) cycle as represented by the following graphic.

The arrows going around the circle in a clockwise direction in this diagram represent the Nourishing Cycle. Each of the elements is nourished by, or produced by, the element that comes before it on the circle.

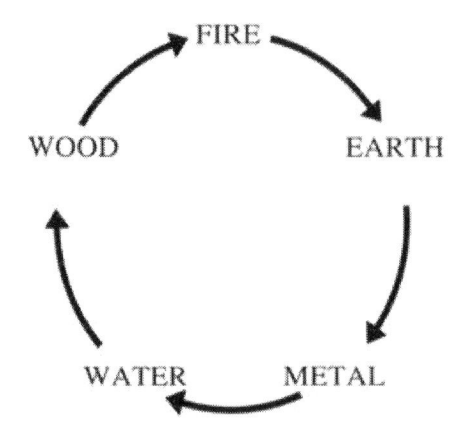

```
         FIRE
       ↗      ↘
   WOOD        EARTH
     ↑          ↓
      ↖        ↙
    WATER    METAL
         ←
```

- Fire burns down to ash and produces earth
- Earth produces Metal in the form of ore
- Metal produces Water when the moisture in the air condenses
- Water is instrumental in the growing process of Wood
- Wood becomes fuel to nourish Fire

We are frequently working with this concept in Feng Shui. When you want to add Fire energy to your environment you can either add an object or color that holds Fire energy or you can enhance the Fire already in the area by adding more Wood energy to provide fuel for the Fire.

Chi Thought: *Energy cannot be produced or destroyed; it can only be transformed.*

Once you understand the concept of this Nourishing Cycle, it is easier to understand the Exhausting cycle. When one element produces another element in the Nourishing Cycle, this will exhaust the element that produced it. For example; we pull metal from the earth in the form of ore. The act of mining this ore exhausts or depletes the earth, leaving it weaker. The following graphic represents this cycle for us.

THE EXHAUSTING CYCLE

When you read counterclockwise around the circle above, you will see how the Exhausting Cycle works.

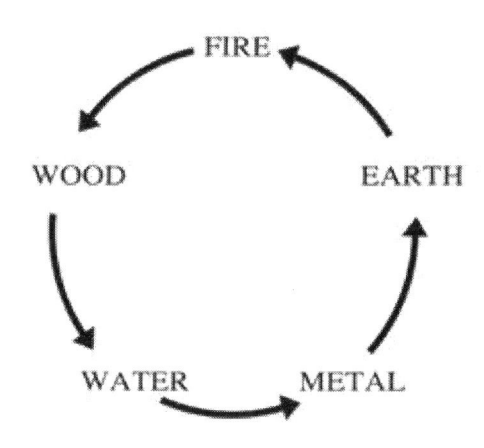

```
        FIRE
      ↙      ↖
  WOOD        EARTH
    ↓          ↑
  WATER  →  METAL
```

- Earth exhausts or puts out Fire
- Metal exhausts or weakens Earth
- Water exhausts or corrodes Metal
- Wood exhausts or drains Water
- Fire exhausts or consumes Wood

This cycle can also be used in Feng Shui to create harmony in your environment. When the harmony is upset by an overabundance of one element, you can get it back into balance by adding the element that exhausts it.

One example of when you would use this technique is if you can't reduce the amount of the overpowering element for practical reasons. For example, if you had too much Fire energy in your kitchen, it would not be practical to reduce that by getting rid of the stove. Instead you can add colors and objects of the Earth element to reduce that excess Fire energy by exhausting it.

The Nourishing (or Productive) cycle and the Exhausting (or Depleting) cycle are the two basic ways that the 5 Elements relate to each other. Now that you understand how those two cycles work, it is time for us to look at the Controlling cycle.

THE CONTROLLING CYCLE

Follow the arrows on this graphic to understand the Controlling Cycle of the elements.

```
        FIRE

WOOD            EARTH


   WATER    METAL
```

- Fire melts Metal
- Earth dams up, or absorbs Water
- Metal cuts Wood
- Water puts out or controls Fire
- Wood (roots) disturbs the Earth

Some texts will refer to this as the destructive cycle, which is certainly accurate but often misunderstood. Although it is an adversarial relationship, this interaction ultimately works to the benefit of all. Think of how a controlled burn in the wilderness clears out the overgrown brush and gives the trees in a forest the right conditions to grow and flourish. Sometimes destruction or control of an element is necessary, like when we use water to douse a fire that is threatening our home. When you are working with a Controlling cycle, the key is to understand what kind of energy you want to generate. If you have an over-abundance of Fire energy, your first thought might be to douse it with water. This will certainly reduce the amount of Fire energy, but it also produces an energy pattern that is full of conflict. For this reason, you should first make an attempt to reduce the Fire energy by withdrawing its source of nourishment (Wood) or by increasing the element that exhausts it (Earth). These techniques will reduce the amount of Fire energy without producing the conflict.

These three cycles form the basic concept we are working with, but there are two more relationship cycles to look at now. The first of these is the Compatible cycle which we will demonstrate using the Nourishing cycle graphic.

COMPATIBLE ELEMENTS

Pick any element on the diagram below. The two elements closest to it on each side are its compatible elements. It will be easy to remember if you think of an element being able to put its arms around the elements it is compatible with. The element in the center of this trio is compatible with the elements on either side, although those two are not compatible with each other.

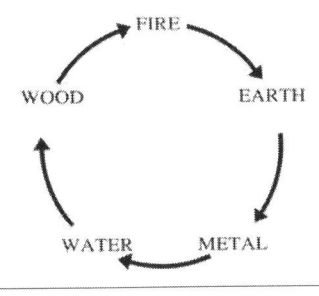

- Fire is compatible with Wood and Earth
- Earth is compatible with Fire and Metal
- Metal is compatible with Earth and Water
- Water is compatible with Metal and Wood
- Wood is compatible with Water and Fire

You will use these relationships in your Feng Shui practice when you want to maintain a tranquil, harmonious environment and the elements are already in balance. If the balance is just right in your living room and you are going to bring in another upholstered chair, you will want to choose a color that is compatible on an elemental level with what you have already created.

The last relationship cycle we are going to look at is one that you will use most often as you apply the principles of Feng Shui to your home or to that of your clients. This is the Balancing cycle of the elements shown by the following graphic where the Controlling cycle and the Nourishing cycle are combined

This graphic is a symbolic representation of how the elements relate to one another in every combination. Once you complete this section, you will be able to simply refer to this combined symbol to know how to adjust the balance of elements in your home or office.

BALANCING ELEMENTS

Choose any element on this graphic; the element directly across is the element that dominates that element.

To balance elements in the dominating, or Controlling cycle, use the element that falls between them on the outer circle. For example, if you chose Fire, the element across the circle would be Water. Water dominates Fire. On the outer circle Wood appears in between Water and Fire. To balance the conflict created by Water and Fire energy, add the Wood element.

To test your grasp of this concept, see if you can determine the balancing element in each the conflicting pairs listed here.

Pair 1 – Fire and Water

Pair 2 – Water and Earth

Pair 3 – Metal and Wood

The answers follow, but don't look until you see how well you can do.

[Answers: 1=wood/2=metal/3=water]

After reading all everything leading up to this question, you probably got all of the answers right. However, do you understand why this element balances the conflict between the other two? If you don't see why this works, review the chapters in this section on the Nourishing cycle and the Exhausting cycle. You should then be able to see how these elements balance the two elements that are in conflict. Using the first pair, Fire and Water, as an example you will see that on the Controlling cycle graphic, Water dominates Fire. (Notice that the point on the arrow between them points to fire showing which element is controlled.) To bring them back into balance we want to weaken Water and strengthen Fire. To weaken water, we look to the Exhausting cycle and see that Wood exhausts Water. To strengthen Fire, we look to the Nourishing cycle graphic and see that Wood feeds Fire.

Wood is our balancing element in this example because Wood will both weaken Water (the dominating element in this pair) and strengthen Fire (the element being dominated) making it a more even match. Now that you have another way of remembering the balancing element, see how well you do on these pairs.

The answers are below, but don't look until you see how well you can do.

Pair 1- Earth and Water

Pair 2- Metal and Fire

Pair 3- Wood and Earth

[Answers: 1=Metal/2=Earth/3=Fire]

The concept you are working on now is one of the most important ones in this book. This is one of the key foundations of Feng Shui and you will want come back to read the material again as you start using the principles of Feng Shui to your daily life and want to come up with ways to improve the harmony in a particular area of your home. The following section will show you what aspect of your life those areas represent.

INTRODUCTION TO THE BAGUA

THE BAGUA IS AN EIGHT-SIDED MAP THAT REPRESENTS THE ONENESS OF LIFE.

Every aspect of your life is anchored energetically somewhere in your home. Nowhere is this concept more clearly defined than in the ancient art of Feng Shui. The Bagua energy map is an octagon. In Chinese "ba" means eight and "gua" means section. When used by a Feng Shui practitioner, the Bagua actually shows nine sections because the center holds energy of its own.

Superimpose the Bagua map (with the edge labeled Fame towards the south) over any floorplan or land plot to discover which aspects of your life are anchored in what locations. The area in the center (This would be approximately 1/9th of the total area) represents your health and unity. Each of these nine areas is referred to as a "Corner" in Feng Shui regardless of its shape. To get the most accurate representation of where each area falls in your living space, you will need a compass. Begin with a scale drawing of your floor plan and place the point of the compass in the exact center of the space. Open the compass to draw a circle around the floor plan making sure that the entire space falls within that circle. The edge of the circle should touch the corner of the wall that extends the farthest. Next divide the circle into twelve equal parts; each of these will contain 30 degrees of the entire area. Align the circle with the cardinal directions [North, South, East and West] and allot 60 degrees (or two pieces of the pie) to each of the cardinal directions. The other four areas will get 30 degrees each to make up the entire 360 degree circle. It is done this way because the energy coming from the cardinal directions is more powerful and its influence will extend further.

Another way to view this energy map is to divide your space into 9 equal sections using a grid pattern. The Bagua interpretations would then look like the grid shown at the end of this paragraph. This method is not as exact, but it is a quick way to get your bearings in a new place. Here the Bagua is basically a grid that is laid over your floor plan to show you which parts of your space correspond to which areas of your life. You can apply this grid to an area as large as a city or as small as your desk top. Each square of the grid has a color, an element, and a number. The energies from these will enhance the life purpose governed by that direction. You can draw this on a sheet of vellum or other sheer paper to make it easy to overlay the floorplan you are working with. This grid is the best alternative to use when applying Feng Shui to a small area, such as a desk top, where external energies are so much farther away that the energy of a person sitting at the desk will actually override them.

BAGUA GRID MAP

4	9	2
3	5	7
8	1	6

Simply take the floor plan of your house (or the room you are working on) and divide it into nine equal squares like those on the grid to see where each numbered square applies to a section of your home. (Keep in mind that the cardinal directions will affect a larger area than the other corners.) The Bagua applies to each room of your house as well as the house itself, but where a particular Feng Shui corner is found in your house will be more important. The correspondences listed at the end of this chapter match up with both the numbers on the grid and the numbers shown on the Bagua map.

MISSING CORNERS

There is a special situation to consider when mapping your house with the Bagua. Not every house or apartment is a simple square or rectangle. Many times there is a section that juts out further than the main residence. If this section is no more than 1/3 of the length of the wall, it would be considered to be an oversized corner in that portion of the Bagua. For example if the room ruts out in the southeast corner, you would have an extended Wealth corner. The shaded grid maps that follow will illustrate this.

When it covers only 1/3 of the length of the wall, that area would be considered an extended corner and give you more opportunities in the aspect of your life it corresponds with.

When choosing a home, keep in mind that there will be a strong focus on this area of your life while living there. In this example that would be the Wealth Corner.

EXTENDED CORNER

4	9	2
3	5	7
8	1	6

If the extension covered at least 2/3 of the length of the wall the area it didn't reach would be a Missing Corner. In this example that would be your Relationship corner.

MISSING CORNER

4	9	2
3	5	7
8	1	6

Any missing corner can be an issue, but this is especially critical if it is one of your power corners (Relationships, Wealth or Career) or if it corresponds with another life aspect that is particularly important to you. When this happens you can take measures to counteract the effect. For example, on the ground floor, you can create a special garden or patio to fill out this corner. A boundary marker such as a fence, hedge, or even a string of twinkling holiday lights would energetically separate this area from the surrounding yard and attach it energetically to the house. Replacing the grass with paving stones or wooden decking would have the same effect. Make an effort to use some Feng Shui friendly design choices to enhance the corner affected. For example if this is your Wealth corner, you might install a fountain or other water feature to symbolize prosperity. For a missing Relationship corner you might add a cozy table for two or a wrought iron loveseat.

Think back to other places you have lived and picture the area this part of the Bagua represented. If you consistently buy or rent property with a missing corner in the Wealth area, you may unconsciously believe that you do not deserve prosperity, or that it is not safe to have abundance. If it was a missing Relationship corner, you may have some ambivalence in that area. The same idea applies to all area of the Bagua and exploring your past choices in living spaces can be a mind-opening exercise.

The following list of correspondences shows where all of the life aspects are anchored energetically your home.

Top Row:

WEALTH/PROSPERITY

Direction: Southeast
Color: Purple
Number: 4
Element: Wood

Corresponds with the blessings of life including material abundance and good fortune

FAME/ILLUMINATION

Direction: South
Color: Red
Number: 9
Element: Fire

Corresponds with recognition, appreciation, reputation; luck, community and moving forward

RELATIONSHIPS

Direction: Southwest
Color: Pink
Number: 2
Element: Earth
Corresponds with marriage, love and intimacy, committed partnerships

Middle Row:

FAMILY

Direction: East
Color: Green
Number: 3
Element: Wood
Corresponds with family relations, longevity, personal growth & ancestors

HEALTH

Direction: Center
Color: Yellow
Number: 5
Element: Earth
Corresponds with the core of your being and balance in all areas of your life as well as your physical and mental health

CHILDREN/CREATIVITY

Direction: West
Color: White
Number: 7
Element: Metal
Corresponds with children, creative projects, anything you "give birth to"

Bottom row:

KNOWLEDGE

Direction: Northeast
Color: Blue
Number: 8
Element: Earth
Corresponds with education, self-contemplation, learning and insight

CAREER OR PATH IN LIFE

Direction: North
Color: Black
Number: 1
Element: Water
Corresponds with your job, occupation, calling or the path you take in life

HELPFUL PEOPLE

Direction: Northwest
Color: Gray
Number: 6
Element: Metal
Corresponds with friends, benefactors, angels and guides as well as travel, communications and interests outside the home (hobbies)

The following section covers each of these areas in more depth and will give you come suggestions on how you can work with the energy in these Feng Shui corners in a way that will attract more of what you would like to see in your life.

WEALTH/PROSPERITY

MONEY, PROPERTY, ANYTHING THAT MAKES LIFE RICHER

Your wealth and prosperity are anchored energetically in the southeast part of your home. The right balance of energy in this area will stimulate the flow of money in your life and make it easy for you to satisfy all of your material desires. This area governs not only personal finances, cash and property, but all of the things that make life richer.

The area of the southeast is related to Wood energy. It is upward, expanding and creates the right environment for growth. Purple is the primary color that resonates with this area, and the secondary colors are red and green.

PERSONAL WORTH

We all receive rewards at a level that reflects the image that we project. This is an extension of a very basic law of nature about exchange for value. If you work in an office, your paycheck reflects the value your employer has placed on you; what you contribute to the company and what the going rate is for that contribution in your community.

Answering telephones requires less education and less of a training investment than writing computer-programming code. The employees in the computer division are going to be offered a higher pay scale than the employees of the same firm who work in customer service. Programmers put a higher value on themselves because they know what it takes to learn their craft. They project a much higher salary requirement, and they get it.

The next level of this decision is based on how you, personally, compare to the other job applicants and employees in your same area. If you work a little harder and learn a little faster than the average employee, your paycheck will reflect the value that your employer places on that competence. However, if you work as an accountant, you will not be paid more because you can play the piano better than your peers. Your employer does not benefit from that talent and it does nothing for his bottom line.

Raises are also based on less tangible expressions of value like the perception of how much you care about your job and the company. On any level, you receive the amount of compensation that reflects your real and perceived value as an employee.

YOU ARE IN CONTROL

You have control over both your real and your perceived value. When you value yourself more, you will be compensated at a higher level. You have a lot of control over what value you project. If you spent four years in college to get a degree in your field, but you do not list that degree on your application, you lower your own value. If you have a bad attendance record, even if you produce more work than anyone else in the department, you will not receive the compensation your work habits would otherwise merit. You are sending out one message and then contradicting it with another message.

I use these examples because I think most people can relate to them. It is harder to make this point with an example about money because almost everyone has attached so much emotional baggage to their feelings about money that it is hard to know what their real feelings are. The principles however, are the same when you apply them to any type of prosperity. Feng Shui will show you how to interpret and improve the message that your personal environment is sending out about how much you are worth.

SENDING MESSAGES

If you have an old, broken-down sofa with ripped and stained upholstery in your family room you might tell people; "this is good enough for now," but you have a problem here. Namely, the Universe does not recognize time. Time is an artificial concept of the material world and the only part of your message that will be acted on is the part that says, "This is good enough."

If you continually say "I can't afford it," you will get your wish; you will never be able to afford it. Notice that when you say something like this, you usually say it with conviction and the feelings behind it are very strong. Compare this to the recommendations for positive affirmations. If you want to benefit from an affirmation, you have to personalize it, state it with conviction and have a strong feeling about it.

Surround yourself with people who love you because the other people in your life help to create your personal reality. Surround yourself with things that you love in your home, and you will set up an energetic pattern that will attract more of the same.

FAME/REPUTATION

FORWARD MOVEMENT, LUCK, RECOGNITION, APPRECIATION

Your fame and recognition are anchored energetically in the south corner of your home. The right balance of energy in this area will ensure that you receive the proper recognition and appreciation for the contributions that you make both in business and in your personal life. This area also influences your reputation in the community, your future prospects and the type and amount of luck that comes your way.

The natural energy patterns of the south relate to summer, midday and full sun. To recreate this energy pattern in your Fame sector; make sure that it is full of light. If you are fortunate enough to have natural light in this area, always be sure that your windows are sparkling clean and repair any cracks or chips immediately. Look at what is outside the windows and minimize anything that interferes with a clear and unobstructed view. If your windows are dirty or blocked, you will have a less than shining reputation and may be the victim of gossip or slander. If trees or bushes block the windows, you may have trouble getting the recognition and appreciation that you deserve.

In both your home and office environments, the south wall is the ideal place for displaying any awards you may have earned. To make your dreams come true faster; you can put objects in this corner to symbolize what you would like to be known for. If you have an entry door in the south, whether at home or at work, it is especially important to have it clear and well lit. Make the path leading up to the door as attractive and inviting as possible and have big, bold address numbers to announce your presence.

Because the Fame corner is associated with the Fire element, you can enhance the energy of the area by using candles or up-lighting. If your light fixtures are spreading light down instead of up, an easy remedy is to fit them with the type of lightbulb that is painted silver on the bottom half – these direct the majority of the light upward. Speaking of lightbulbs, you can always have Fire energy in this area if you put a red bulb in a nightlight fixture and leave it burning around the clock.

You will want to enhance the energy in your Fame area if you are hoping to be considered for a promotion at work, if you are running for political office, or if you have started up a new enterprise. To enhance your Fame, keep the lights burning around the clock in this area for the entire time that you are awaiting the outcome of a decision about matters like those just mentioned. The Feng Shui remedies used most effectively in the Fame area include light, candles, bells or chimes and faux firecrackers (or other noise-makers.) The firecrackers are to announce you to the world and the bells or chimes will call attention to your true worth. When you are using color to enhance this area, chose something from the red family. You can choose orange, burgundy or any of the shades found in a candle flame. Red is a very powerful color and you only need to use a little bit.

Don't make the mistake of thinking that only celebrities or public figures need to pay attention to the Fame corner. Fame and reputation cover not only your visibility – for example the plumber or real estate agent that comes to mind when someone is asked for a recommendation, but your reputation is well. A good reputation could well make you the first person who comes to mind when it comes to a job promotion, a public office nomination or even an upgrade to first class on an airplane.

If you do not feel properly appreciated or recognized in this world, look at your Fame corner with Feng Shui eyes to see if you are working around any obstacles or limitations.

RELATIONSHIPS

MARRIAGE, LOVE AND INTIMATE CONNECTIONS

Look at the southwest corner to find the Relationship area of your home. When things are in harmony, the energy in this area will help you attract new relationships and improve the ones you have. The Relationship corner is also referred to as the marriage corner and it governs intimate, committed, one-on-one relationships. You have other relationships (family, children, business people, and friends) but these energies are anchored elsewhere in the Bagua. The Relationship corner is considered the second most important one of your power corners in Feng Shui. This is located in the southwest part of your home, and it resonates with Earth energy and shades of red and pink. The three power corners of Wealth, Career and Relationships are sometimes referred to as the Lucky Trinity because if things are working well for you in these three areas of your life, you are certain to attract good luck in every other part of your life as well.

THE THINGS WE DO FOR LOVE

Your choices of colors, materials, and shapes in the Relationship area will determine whether or not your décor will increase the energy of this area or diminish it. The colors to use if you want to increase the flow of loving energy around you are red and pink. Appropriate colors also include mauve, ivory or apricot. Use any variation of flesh tones that appeal to you and fit in with your decorating scheme. You should note that there are some subtle differences in the types of energy these colors draw in.

For example, pink is a strong, supportive, loving energy while red will bring in more passion. You may want to add small touches of red to your bedroom décor to increase the energy in a marriage that has gone stale, but too much emphasis on red can bring you the kind of hot, passionate love that burns out quickly. If you feel the need to stabilize your marriage, or keep a mate from wandering, minimize your use of this color. Red is a very powerful color and a little bit goes a long way. Apricot is a color that resonates with an energy that will attract new love, but once you find that love, switch to pink or the love you have found may start to wander.

There are other differences in the approach you should use if you are trying to hold on to and strengthen a relationship rather than attract a new one. If you want stability in your relationship, find a way to add heavy, stable, objects to your room arrangement. Urns and statues work well, and so do bookends. Bookends are not only heavy, but the come in pairs. Not surprisingly, two is the number associated with the relationship corner, and to attract more love into your life you need to think in pairs. Use a pair of candlesticks rather than one large candleholder, or display a pair of pictures instead of one big one. Avoid any pictures of solitary figures, or you may become one.

AND WHAT WE SHOULDN'T DO

Your bedroom furniture should be arranged in a way that emphasizes the union of two people in this space, even when one of those people has yet to appear. If you sleep in a single bed because you don't need a double bed yet, you just might be guaranteeing that you never will need one. If you are sharing your bedroom with a partner and want to avoid marital or relationship conflicts, give both sides of your bed equal treatment. Placing the bed with one side flush against the wall will also set the stage for inequality in a relationship. Each side of the bed should have its own nightstand or equivalent and equal access to lights, alarm clocks, etc. If these objects are within easy reach of one bed partner and the other partner has to get out of bed to turn on the lamp or turn off the alarm, it will lead to conflicts and power struggles within the relationship.

Anything and everything that resonates with the energy of a previous relationship should be removed to leave room for a new relationship to come in. There should not even be any pictures of a former spouse in the dresser drawers, let alone on display. In addition, while we are on the subject of photos, don't keep pictures of your children in the bedroom either. You want this to be your personal sanctuary where you temporarily forget your role as a parent.

The overall energy of the bedroom should honor its intended purpose as a place reserved for rest and intimacy. This means no TV, exercise equipment, ironing board or other unrelated items in the room. You will enjoy the most restful kind of sleep if you keep electrical equipment in your bedroom to a bare minimum, and none of it should be less than 6 feet from your head as you sleep. This means that you might need to use a wind-up clock rather than an electric one. If you heat the bed with an electric blanket, pre-heat your bed and then turn the blanket off before going to sleep.

FAMILY/GROWTH

ELDERS, GROWTH, SELF-IMPROVEMENT, AUTHORITY FIGURES

The Family area is located in the East section of your home. This area represents the nuclear family as well as your birth family. It governs your relationship to your parents and other authority figures and even ancestral relationships. If you are having trouble with your boss or the zoning board, look to this area to read your unconscious signals. Because families are the growth unit of our world, it is appropriate that this area also governs your personal growth. You will want to give special attention with to this area any time you are trying to break a bad habit, establish a healthy one, or have any self-improvement plans. If you have clutter in this part of your house, you will probably find that you also have obstacles and limitations when it comes to personal growth. The Family corner in Feng Shui resonates with the color green, the number 3, the element of wood, and the energy of thunder. This life-station is associated with spring, sunrise and new beginnings.

GROWTH AND HARMONY

Regardless of whether you are striving for personal growth or family harmony, here is a traditional Feng Shui ritual that can help you create the right energy in this area to ensure success. Select a lush, healthy, green plant – a Jade plant would be the traditional choice – and pot it in an attractive container. Place the container in the east part of your house and state your intentions as you put it into place. Now each time you water the plant, you will be reinforcing those intentions.

If the plant becomes straggly, or dies, you should immediately replace it with one that is even larger and more beautiful. Watch to see when the plant begins to outgrow its container and re-pot it when necessary. The plant will serve as a constant reminder of how you are growing too.

FAMILY SPIRIT

If you would like to achieve greater family harmony in your life, enhancing the East sector of your home is the place to start. This is the area of the home that will benefit the most from a display of family photographs or keepsakes. Because this is the area that governs our ancestors, this would be an extremely favorable location to display your family heirlooms.

In the practice of traditional Feng Shui, the doors in a house symbolize the parents and the windows symbolize the children. Therefore in a house that has a disproportionate number of windows to the number of doors (the rule of thumb is 3 windows for each door) there is a danger than the children in the home will be unruly and disrespectful.

If you have a house like this, it is usually not practical to add a door or remove some windows. What you can do however, is symbolically close off some of the windows with drapes or shutters. In traditional Feng Shui, this is the area governed by the Green Dragon. Ideally, the East side of your space will have some type of natural barrier between the edge of your property and the beginning of your neighbor's property. If this side is unprotected you may soon find that your resources are being drained. In the Form School method of Feng Shui, a consultant would search for a building site that had a natural form of protection on the East side. This could be low hills or mature trees or even another building. In today's world, you will most likely have to make the best out of whatever land you are living on now, but that does not mean that you can't remedy this situation using Feng Shui. If you want to create Green Dragon energy you can build a fence or plant a hedge. If the amount of space does not allow for one of these solutions, see if you can add a flower bed and form a symbolic boundary that is both protective and beautiful.

HEALTH

PHYSICAL HEALTH, WELL-BEING, VITALITY, UNITY

This part of the Bagua influences primarily your physical health, but also your mental, emotional and spiritual health. For this reason, the Health Corner, which is located in the center of your space, is considered the most important area of your home. The energy in the center of your home radiates out into all the rest of your space. There is no way you can enhance any of the other corners when the central one is not balanced. This area should be as clear as possible and well-lit. If natural light is not abundant, supplement it with artificial light, perhaps even a chandelier.

In our society, most of us are starving for balance in our lives. Urban living takes us further and further from nature, which adds to the stress we already feel from the fast pace of modern life. You should never underestimate the impact of your environment on your health. There are the basic issues like air exchange, cleanliness and sanitation, but good Feng Shui practices can help you achieve health benefits above and beyond the basics.

Feng Shui is the art of balancing and harmonizing the energy in your personal environment to create beneficial changes in your life. A well-balanced environment will enhance the free flow of energy in your space, which will result in better health and well-being as well as more prosperity, love and happiness. The Chinese know that if you have your health, you have everything and without your health you have nothing.

A lack of balance in your personal environment can show up as fatigue, lethargy and depression at one end of the spectrum; or as high blood pressure, tension and thinly suppressed anger at the other end. Depression and its offshoots are symptoms of low level energy, stagnant energy or energy that is excessively Yin. Energy that is excessively Yang or energy that moves too quickly will result in the symptoms described at the other end of the spectrum.

LOW ENERGY CURES

Let us use examples from each end of the spectrum to see how this works. On one end, we have depression, and its milder varieties of sadness, fatigue and boredom. All of these are examples of slow moving or stagnant energy.

Energy enters our homes through the front door, and to a lesser extent, through the windows. Energy leaves through the back door, completing the process. If there are any obstructions at your front entrance, it will reduce the amount of energy you have coming in. Windows that are blocked, broken or dirty will also lower the amount and quality of energy you receive. If you do not have a back door in your home or apartment, the energy does not have an easy exit after it is depleted. When the stale energy cannot move out, there is no room for fresh energy to come in. Keep your back door in good repair and free of obstructions. If you do not have a back door, the depleted energy can exit through windows or you can create your own energy patterns through furniture placement and other Feng Shui remedies.

To raise the energy of your space, lift things up physically. If you are storing anything on the floor, move it to tabletop height, or put it on a shelf if possible. Then check for the general direction of lines in your space. Hanging plants, trailing vines, window swags and floor length tablecloths all create low level energy because they bring your attention downward. Introduce more light in the form of spotlights or accent lamps. Mirrors will increase energy too, just place them carefully so that they will reflect something positive. Add sound either physically or symbolically with wind chimes or artwork depicting music. Living things such as plants or animals also introduce energy. And most importantly; use the space. Often when energy is stagnating, it is because you are not using that part of your home. If you have a room that you seldom use, put an aquarium or a house plant in the room so you will be entering it on a regular basis to care for this addition.

REMEDIES FOR EXCESSIVE ENERGY

At the other end of the spectrum, we encounter frayed nerves, high blood pressure and anger always just below the surface. These are symptoms of excess energy, or energy that is moving too fast. In this case, you need to slow down the energy that enters your space and let it collect and linger long enough to nourish you. To calm the energy, reduce the number of Yang elements in your space or increase the Yin elements.

Control excess light in your space by covering broad expanses of glass with curtains or shades. Avoid harsh overhead lighting and use table lamps if possible. Limit the number of green plants to no more than one or two; an excess of plants can create an excess of energy. And choose ones with round, broad leaves rather than spiky ones. Check to see if you have too many mirrors for the amount of space, and do not place two mirrors so that they are reflecting one another. Cover some of the hard surfaces with fabric or soften the harsh lines of a chair or sofa by adding a decorative pillow or afghan. Replace artwork depicting battle scenes or speeding objects with tranquil scenes. Make sure the seating you use is not in a direct line with the door as the incoming energy should approach you softly and not head on.

Try some of the suggestions that appeal to you and see what a difference these simple changes can make in the overall energy of your personal space. The changes you make on the outside will soon be reflected on the inside resulting in better health and increased vitality.

CHILDREN/CREATIVITY

FERTILITY, ORIGINALITY, INVENTIVENESS

In the west part of your home, you will find the Children's corner. This location influences your relationship with any children in the house. If you want more harmony in your relationship with your children, work on the west corner. If you have trouble conceiving a child, look this area over very carefully for any blockages.

Moreover, this location influences the child in all of us. Work on this area if you want to get in touch with the creativity and originality that you enjoyed as a child. If you find yourself falling into the same patterns time after time, you can use the energy of this area to help yourself find new and innovative ways of dealing with your problems.

This is a naturally Yang area, corresponding to the color white or any of the metallic colors. The area is associated with the compass direction west, the number 7, sunset, fall and Metal energy. This is a great placement for a television, stereo system or personal computer, as all of these carry lots of Metal energy.

Clocks also give off Metal energy, as do metallic frames around pictures and mirrors. This is not a good area to place a water feature or too much wood energy. If your décor does not lend itself to actual metal, or if you are using the location for a child's bedroom, use sound or movement remedies to enhance the area.

THE SPARK OF LIFE

People who do not have children or any immediate plans to start a family, will sometimes overlook the Children's/Creativity area of their homes. Although bringing forth a new life could easily be considered the supreme act of creation, it is certainly not the only one. Anything that we give life to is anchored energetically in this section of the Bagua.

You might be giving life to the character in a play you are part of, or in a novel you are writing. Or you might conceive of a new way to regulate landfills. These activities are all equally creative. It is no accident that we use words like conceive or create when talking about these endeavors. Or that we will refer to a pet project as "my baby". These things would not exist if we did not create them.

When arranging the décor in this part of your house, find ways to give it the playful atmosphere of children's energy. Moving objects like a windsock, mobile or wind chime, are good remedies for stagnant energy in the west.

HARNESSING CHILDREN'S ENERGY

If you are trying to conceive a child, or if you already have children, this area should be dedicated to them. If it is not a part of your home that would lend itself to a nursery, playroom or child's bedroom, at least make sure that your children are well represented here. This is the place to display their school photographs as well as all those works of art that they bring home over the years.

This is also a great part of your home in which to sit and daydream. After all, what is more creative than our thoughts? Our thoughts are so powerful that they actually create the circumstances of our lives. It is the way we think about ourselves, the way we think about other people and the way we think about our life circumstances that creates our reality.

CREATIVE ARTS

Those of you who would like to express yourselves through the arts should be particularly attentive to this section of the Bagua. Whether you are drawn to music, dance, painting or the written word, you can remove your creative blocks by enhancing the energy in your Children's Corner. Think about using this area for a dance studio, or as the setting for your typewriter stand, or your easel. Or perhaps install a comfortable chair where you can just sit quietly and wait for the muse to inspire you.

Low creativity may be the missing ingredient when you are experiencing challenges in other areas of your life as well. If you are not enjoying the level of prosperity that you desire, perhaps you are overlooking some income opportunities you had not seen before. If your intimate relationships are not as dynamic and fulfilling as you would like them to be, boosting your creativity just might provide you with some new solutions to old problems. Creativity is what puts the spark of life into every aspect of our existence.

When you make the effort to energize your Children's Corner, you can use the creative mind you had as a child with the wisdom and experience you have gained as an adult for an extremely powerful combination. So unleash the child in yourself! Your Creativity Corner is where you can envision your fantasy and watch it come true.

KNOWLEDGE

WISDOM, ACADEMIC ACHIEVEMENT, SELF-CULTIVATION

The northeast section of your space is the area of Knowledge and Self-cultivation. It is associated with wisdom, education and academic achievement, as well as the process of getting to know yourself better. This corner of the Bagua resonates with an energy pattern that is conducive to clear thinking and focused concentration. The energy of this area is perfect for a desk, study or meditation spot. If you keep this area uplifted, it will be easier for you to learn quickly and to retain what you have learned.

When there are no students living in your household and you are out of school yourself, it is easy to think that you do not have a reason to concern yourself with the energy in your Knowledge Corner. Although you may not be a student, there are times when you need learn quickly and retain what you learn. There are times in both your business and personal life when you can benefit from the ability to think clearly and decisively.

In Feng Shui every aspect of your life is anchored energetically somewhere in your home. When you need to focus your concentration to learn quickly and retain what you learn, it is important to enhance this part of your living space. Having the right kind of energy in your Knowledge area will lead to:

- Coherent brainwaves
- Creative thinking
- Longer attention span
- Better learning ability
- Better recall

When your children are trying to get into college, or when your spouse is trying to pass the bar exam, academics become very important in your household. When you are at this stage of life, you will do well to set up a study or desk area in the northeast part of your home if possible. If this is not feasible, you should try to put the desk in the northeast corner of whatever room is used for studying. A clean desk has been proven to increase your productivity, creativity, and even your raise your level of job satisfaction. Both at home and at work, you should clear off your desk every night before you leave. This way you will come in to a fresh start each morning, and feel like you are in control. If you *feel* that you are in control, you will be.

THOUGHTFUL REMEDIES

Try not to have your back to the door when you are working at the desk. If you cannot avoid this, have a mirror on the wall in front of you (or attached to your computer monitor) so that you can be aware of any activity behind you without interrupting your work. To further enhance your powers of concentration and increase your attention span, the traditional Feng Shui cure is to hang a faceted crystal over the desk. To make this remedy even more powerful, hang the crystal by a red silk cord.

This remedy is also an effective way to focus your concentration and promote inner tranquility when you are using your Knowledge Corner for meditation or inner work. This life-station in the northeast part of your living space covers not only wisdom and academic achievement, but also inner wisdom, contemplation and self-cultivation.

Mental Focus – that is to say, what you pay attention to, what you think about, what you visualize and what you say to yourself – determines the circumstances of your life. Feng Shui will help you direct your thoughts in a pattern that can and will bring about beneficial changes in your life. Making the decision to focus on the Knowledge Corner of your home is the first step in that process.

CAREER

OCCUPATION, BUSINESS, LIFE PURPOSE, CALLING

Understanding and achieving your purpose in life is a vital key to personal balance. Discovering what you were meant to do is one of life's most important questions and it will surface again and again as you move from one stage of life to another. The Career life-station of the Bagua governs not only the occupation from which you derive a living, but also your purpose in life. For most of us the key ingredient to a happy life is a meaningful job that pays the bills.

Perhaps you have reached the age where you have achieved everything you want in your professional field and are now wondering what comes next. You should activate the energy in your Career Corner at this stage as well as when you are job hunting, changing fields or looking for advancement in your current job. You should also focus on this area if there is a lot of turmoil where you work or if you would like to be selected for a volunteer position outside of your profession. By activating the energy in your Career Corner, you are projecting the message that you are open to recognizing your true calling and that you are ready to attract positive new experiences.

Your Career energy is anchored in the north part of your home. There is also a Career corner in each room of your house; the most important ones are in your living room and in your home office. When you are focusing on the career aspects of your life you will want to look at all of these to make sure that you are not sabotaging your own efforts. Anything in this area that is broken or that needs cleaning, or repairs is a signal that something is not working in this part of your life. If the area is cluttered, you are choking off the flow of career opportunities in your life, so you will want to get rid of anything in your Career corner that you don't absolutely love or absolutely need.

CAREER SYMBOLS

The number associated with this area is one. In your Career Corner it is best to display single objects to resonate with the concept that you alone are responsible for the direction you take in life. (Much like the way you placed things in pairs to symbolize partnership aspects in your Relationship Corner). The Career Corner is in the north, and the element associated with the north is Water. The color representing Water is black, but you can also enhance this area with deep shades of blue, green or purple. Using reflective materials like glass, crystal or mirrors will also symbolize Water, as do objects and furnishings with a wavy or irregular (free-form) shape.

To enhance this Water energy, the strongest remedies you can use would be actual water elements. If practical, you could install an aquarium or indoor fountain here. You could also work with an outdoor fountain in your yard or garden. If you use one of these water remedies, it is very important that you keep the water clean and free-flowing at all times. Although fountains and aquariums are two of the most powerful Feng Shui cures, you are better off without a water feature if you ever let yours become dirty, stagnant or clogged.

ADDING LIFE FORCE

A tortoise is the animal associated with the energy in the north. If keeping a pet turtle appeals to you, you could install a decorative bowl here that is large enough to hold a turtle and a stone that is somewhat larger than the turtle. The water should be deep enough for the animal to submerge itself. Turtles like to spend time both in and out of the water. You can buy feeding pellets at a pet store and supplement that diet with fresh vegetables on occasion. One turtle would be the proper number, and don't worry, turtles are solitary creatures and do not mind being alone. Like other water features, this arrangement is very powerful, but will do you more harm than good if you don't keep it fresh and clean at all times. If a water feature is not practical for you or appropriate to the area, use the colors, shapes and materials that symbolize water or exhibit artwork of water scenes. The best choices would be of moving water, particularly waterfalls.

Like financial status and personal relationships, your career or path in life is an essential area that cannot be separated from who you are as a person. Your Career Corner, together with your Wealth Corner, and your Relationship Corner, make up what are referred to as your Power Corners in Feng Shui. When making adjustments or enhancements to your personal environment, make sure you do not overlook any of these three important areas.

HELPFUL PEOPLE

MENTORS, ANGELS, TRAVEL, INTERESTS OUTSIDE THE HOME

Nobody can hope to have a full and successful life without the help of other people. Pay attention to the northwest section of your home if you want to keep the channels open for help and assistance in your life. Look at the area as it is now to see what unconscious messages you might be projecting. If this area is crowded or cluttered, the message you are projecting is that you don't need any help; you can do it yourself. You are telling the universe that you have everything you need. Don't make the mistake of thinking help comes only in the form of financial benefactors or physical assistance. It will often appear in the form of synchronistic encounters or off-hand remarks that have a special significance for you at a particular time. When we tell the universe that we are open to assistance, we will be helped in any number of ways. Often the universe will use people as a vehicle to deliver the assistance we need. Other times the help can appear in non-human form: a great parking spot or beautiful weather on the day of your outdoor party.

SOURCES OF HELP

Your Helpful People area also represents assistance in the form of guidance and angelic protection. If you let the word go out that you are seeking guidance by opening up your northwest section, guidance will come in the form of dreams, or coincidences that lead you to be in just the right place at the right time. However, in order to hear the advice the universe is happy to send you, you have to be listening. Clutter in your Helpful People area is much like a running conversation in your head that prevents you from recognizing assistance when it does come your way. Metal energy, the color gray, and the number 6 represent this area. This is an excellent place to display pictures of your ancestors if you want to assume their role. The ancestor you want to emulate does not have to be a blood relative. For example, if you want to be a great writer, you could put pictures of Shakespeare or Kafka in this corner. If you have a work colleague you'd like to have as a mentor, you can elicit their help by putting their business card on a silver tray in this area.

CURES AND RITUALS

Here is a traditional cure that operates along these lines. Think of five people whose assistance would help you to accomplish your goals. Visualize exactly how they could help you, and be very specific about it. Now take five pieces of paper and write down the name of the person (or organization) and the specific way in which they could help you. For example, a young man yearning for a medical career might have five slips of paper that look something like this:

> 1.) Harvard Medical School –Will accept me to their program.
> 2.) Aunt Jane – I can stay with her while I am going to school.
> 3.) Medical Alumni– Will offer me used textbooks at no cost.
> 4.) First National Bank – Will grant me a low-cost student loan.
> 5.) John Smith – Will show me the ropes as a freshman.

Read them each day, for 27 days. While visualizing the person whose name is on the slip providing you with the assistance you desire. Then dispose of the papers and put the entire matter out of your mind knowing that you will get what you need. If you need to write letters asking for assistance, or perhaps make telephone calls trying to locate a chaperone for the 4th grade field trip, try to write those letters, or make those calls from the northwest section of your space. If you do this you will be using the energy of the Helpful People corner to your best advantage. An important way to work with this energy is to keep the area clean and clear at all times so that you will know what you want. Equally important is to make sure the area is well lit so that benefactors can find you. The other side of receiving help is giving it. The more energy you put out in the form of support and assistance to others, the more energy of this type you will receive in return. Remember: like attracts like.

BUYING OR SELLING A HOUSE

People don't buy a house, they buy a home. The same things that create a good Feng Shui atmosphere in your own life will make your house feel more like a home to potential buyers. So put yourself in the shoes of a home seeker and conduct the following Feng Shui assessment on the house you want to sell. As you go through, keep a list of the things you observe that could be changed to improve the property.

As you approach the home, where does your eye go? How does it make you feel? Make sure a property you are showing lifts the spirits. If your potential buyer is dragging and tired from looking at too many homes for too long, what will lead to a sale faster than a home that lifts their spirits and makes them feel rejuvenated?

Here you can apply what you have learned about Feng Shui to a real home so you can gain some experience in what you should look for when you want to enhance a property you have listed, or how to make a good decision when buying a new residence. At the end of this section you will find a handy checklist to use when you shopping for a home or are getting a property ready to sell. Eventually these items will become second nature to you, but until then, bringing a copy of this check list with you.

When you find yourself with a hard-to-sell listing, reviewing the Bagua shown below can give you some clues as to which particular area you need to evaluate most closely. If the home shows well, but the money part always seems to fall through, see what is going on in the Wealth Corner. When you find yourself drowning in red tape with lenders, appraisers and other consultants, take a close look at the Helpful People Corner. Every aspect of the sale is anchored energetically somewhere in the house, and before long you will know right where to look regardless of what type of problem you are facing.

EVALUATING A PROPERTY
FIXING WHAT CAN – AVOIDING WHAT YOU CAN'T

For a real estate professional, the first step in evaluating a property is to determine whether or not the seller is actually ready to let go of the house. If the owner is not, they could find themselves expending huge amounts of energy with almost no hope of seeing any return on that investment. If you are selling your own home, don't list it until you have resolved any reservations about selling or moving. If the move has been forced by a job change, divorce or other situation outside your control, this can be a real problem. If you are reluctant to let go of your home you have to resolve this issue in your own mind first. You need to accept the situation and focus on the future. Take some time to say goodbye to your house; thank the house for giving you shelter and sanctuary and for all the good memories that have been created there. When you clear your mind of any ambivalence about selling, you clear the way to a sale.

PREPARING A PROPERTY TO SELL

When strapped with a hard-to-sell property, most sellers and realtors will make frantic efforts to get it moving. If you focus your efforts *before* the listing, you will find that you need to invest significantly less time and money. More importantly, you will not lose any potential buyers by showing them the property before it is in optimal market condition. As motivated seller, you are probably well versed in all of the standard efforts such as fresh paint or instant landscaping, so the following checklist will focus on Feng Shui enhancements that address the energetic readiness of a house.

LEARN TO RECOGNIZE AND REMEDY THESE COMMON ROADBLOCKS TO QUICK SALES

Subtle predecessor energies that make potential buyers feel like they are intruding can kill a sale. Buyers can be put off by family photos, heirlooms or other memorabilia if there are a lot on display. Pack these early, or, if they must be stored on the premises, box them up and store them along the west side of the house. This position resonates with movement. Having these items displayed prominently make it hard for a buyer to imagine themselves living in the house.

Anything heavy, or extremely large, in the "anchor spot", which is the south side of the ground floor, symbolizes the current homeowner's stability and permanence in the home. This will make a buyer more likely to keep looking, just like a man on the prowl will pass over a woman with a big diamond on her ring finger. If you are not taking this item with you, try to sell or give it away before showing the house. If it is a large entertainment unit, perhaps it can be broken up into smaller components as you prepare the house for showing.

When using Feng Shui cures to adjustment specific challenges when selling, it is best to apply remedies to the ground floor as this symbolizes current life, but you should also make some efforts in the corresponding areas of other floors.

EVALUATING THE ENTRANCE
THE APPROACH

A desirable home is a refuge and a sanctuary; does the home you are approaching feel like one? Is the first thing that catches your eye something beautiful and smile provoking? Or is the first thing you notice something that is missing or broken? It creates bad energy to have any empty planters or hanging baskets, etc. around the front (or rear) entrance. Fill them with something, or have them removed. Make certain that all lights are in working condition and the bulbs are not burned out. Also be sure the doorbell works.

In China, a front entrance is traditionally guarded by a pair of Fu Dogs. While this may not fit in with the décor of most western homes, the concept is an easy one to translate. The English version of Fu Dogs would be either Griffins or Lions. You can also flank the entrance with a pair of massive stone urns or topiary trees. You may have already created this feeling with plantings on either side of the front entrance. Or perhaps the architectural details of the home have this guardian feeling built in with columns, railings, or other flanking elements.

The effect can be also achieved with something as simple and practical as a gas light on the left, and a mailbox on the right. For maximum affect, the features should be placed relatively close to the front door (the smaller the objects, the closer they should be) and the more evenly balanced the elements are, the better.

THE FRONT DOOR

Good Chi begins at the front door. Make sure that the entrance is inviting and remove any visible or subliminally perceptible obstacles. This includes cutting back or pruning any encroaching or overhanging bushes or shrubs. Do this even if the greenery does not actually obstruct your path, but appears too close, or simply *feels* like it is in your way.

To create the feeling that this is a very special place, consider the traditional Chinese good luck remedy of painting the front door a different color than any other elements of the house. Check to see that the door opens easily and fully. Creaking hinges, or sticking and scraping on any part of the door will make it as difficult for your client to "get into" the house on a subconscious level as it does on a physical one.

THE FOYER

If you are storing anything behind the door, or using the door or wall behind it to hang hat and coats, be sure to remove these before you show the house. The entire entry hall or foyer should be completely free of clutter to symbolize easy movement from the house to the outside world and vice versa.

Also remove any personal family memorabilia from the entry. Family pictures, school projects or the plaque that reads "The Campbell Clan" are great ways to mark your own turf while you are living in a house, but if you want it to sell; the prospective buyer needs a clean canvas on which to make their own impressions.

Once you enter the door, do you flow easily into the house or do you encounter obstructions? Is there a place (ideally within 10 steps of the door) to put down any packages you might be carrying? This element symbolizes hospitality, and your potential buyers will welcome a house that welcomes them. A mirror is another hospitable touch that makes it possible to make a quick check of one's appearance when coming or going.

SUMMARY OF THE ENTRANCE

Your home should be a sanctuary from the outside world. When you return home, it should feel like the house is putting its arms around you. To create this feeling in a property you are selling, the entrance must be spacious, well lighted and free of any clutter. This is the buffer zone where you shed the stressful energies of the outside world and gather your personal energy in anticipation of shifting into your "at-home" persona. You do not want to be confronted with anything that reminds you of work to be done and this includes things that are missing or broken as well as anything that is less than clean. A first impression is hard to shake, so make it a good one.

Four elements than should be incorporated into the ideal entryway are:

> *A mirror for last minute checking on your way in or out*
> *A place to put down packages or other burdens*
> *A place to sit if you are waiting or if you are removing footwear*
> *A green plant of some kind to give the feeling of bringing the outdoors inside*

Incorporate as many of these elements as possible into a clean, clear, well-lighted entrance and you are half way to escrow.

EVALUATING THE LIVING ROOM

The living room of any house is where your buyers will picture themselves interacting with friends and relatives who are not a part of the immediate family; their "public" so to speak. For this reason the best location for a living room is near the front of the house, preferably overlooking the street in front. The most unfortunate layout you could have is where guest must go through another (more private) part of the house to reach the living room. If you are faced with this situation, you may want to prepare yourself with some practical suggestions on how they could rearrange this space after the sale.

The more outside windows you have in this room, the greater the perception of sociability and visibility. An interior living room area, with few windows, gives a feeling of isolation that needs to be remedied with enhancements such as mirrors, paintings of outdoor scenes and a large amount of light. Unless you have a very undesirable view, try to keep all of the curtains and blinds open when showing this room.

You can also meet this challenge with the generous use of green plants, either live or silk. Absolutely no dried arrangements here or anywhere else in the house! Dried flowers are dead energy and you have to keep things lively if you want to make the sale.

The feeling of openness and visibility we are striving for must not go so far that the client feels exposed or vulnerable. One feature that prevents this is a separate foyer or entrance hall. If you have a listing that does not have either one of these, you can add to appeal of the home by creating a perceived separation between the actual living quarters and the outside world. If you are setting up a reception table for an open house type of showing, try to position it to partially close off the living room and prevent the Chi from either rushing in or rushing out. If the house is still furnished, you can rearrange the furniture to create this effect if you have not already done so.

In Feng Shui terms, what we are trying to create here is the "command position". This would be where the home owner would be able to see anyone entering his space soon enough to react to that presence. If you are using furniture to slow down the movement through the main entrance, be careful not to use what appears to be the most important piece of furniture in the room. This furniture, usually a comfortable chair - should be reserved for the head of the house and placed in the command position.

Furniture should also be grouped into conversational areas rather than lined up around the walls or facing an entertainment center. Make it easy for your client to visualize this as a place to hold harmonious gatherings of friends and family and you will be taking great strides towards giving them that right-at-home feeling that leads to quick sales.

EVALUATING THE DINING ROOM

The dining room is another place where buyers picture themselves socializing with friends and family. Make sure that this room carries a lively, upbeat energy. Open drapes whenever possible, and make sure that the light fixtures are fitted with the appropriate wattage. This room works best when situated in front of the centerline of the house, although proximity to the kitchen is just as important.

In this age of fewer dinner parties, and families going their separate ways at meal time, a formal dining room is often underused. This situation can easily lead to stagnant energy in the dining room which can also seep into other areas of the house. The traditional Feng Shui cures for stagnant energy fall into three main categories; light, sound and movement.

When using light remedies you should work with both natural and artificial lighting. A dining room does not require a lot of privacy, and sheer curtains or half curtains can work very well while letting in the maximum about of light. If the house has window treatments that create a dark and gloomy atmosphere, it may not be practical to change or remove these before a showing – but you can certainly leave them open. Artificial lighting in this room is usually limited to an overhead fixture simply because of the way a dining room is furnished, but adding wall sconces is a huge plus. Candles also work very well in a dining room and bring to mind gracious dining even when they are not lighted.

If you add a centerpiece and a tablecloth or runner to the table, or even complete place settings, it will make it even easier for the buyer to visualize the potential of this room.

Sound energy can be introduced by adding a wind chime if that would fit in with the style of the room; or perhaps you can extend speaker wires from an adjacent living room or den and enjoy some recorded music! Most of the traditional Feng Shui remedies using movement would be inappropriate in a dining room but if you use your imagination, you can create movement with elements that are already in the room. Lightweight curtain material will allow for gently billowing drapes during open window weather, or create a similar feeling when they are stirred as someone passes by. Curtains or drapes that are light in color also create this feeling. There may be room in a corner for a real or silk plant such as a palm tree or fichus tree, and you can create energizing movement by positioning a small, battery operated fan behind the planter to rustle the leaves.

When you can create an inviting atmosphere in the dining room, your buyers are likely to find themselves imaging that this is a house that could bring the family back together at dinner time – and that translates into sales.

EVALUATING THE KITCHEN

Regardless of which area of the Bagua it falls in, the kitchen always represents abundance. Your prosperity is directly related to your ability to "put food on the table." The most potent symbol of wealth in your kitchen is the stove itself. A kitchen located in the south part of the house, or a stove that faces south will create too much Fire energy for comfort or safety. If you encounter this situation, remedy the condition with Earth energy because Earth exhausts Fire. Clients can become overly critical when exposed to an overabundance of Fire energy and this is not conducive to quick sales.

You can introduce Earth into the kitchen by using clay tiles on the floor or countertops. If this is not practical, you can use Earth colors like yellow, brown or tan and shapes that are flat or square. Keep plants out of a kitchen with excess Fire energy because Wood feeds fire. For the same reason, you should minimize green colors and other symbols of wood. You may want to have a small amount of Wood energy in the kitchen however to balance the conflicting energy of Fire and Water that we will cover next.

CONFLICTING ENERGY

You may have noticed that a kitchen is the location in your home where accidents, arguments and other conflicts arise most often. The reason for this is that like attracts like and a kitchen is often filled with conflicting energy in terms of the 5 Elements. This comes about because virtually every kitchen will have both a sink (water energy) and a stove (fire energy). Much of your other cooking equipment, such as a crockpot, waffle iron or coffee brewer will also carry fire energy. Your dishwasher and refrigerator carry water energy.

So how do you balance this conflicting energy? We learned earlier that Wood is the elemental energy that balances this combination. Ideally, the Water elements and the Fire elements in your kitchen will not be located right next to each other or directly across from each other. When you do find this configuration in a kitchen, introduce something of Wood element between the fire and water.

In a kitchen, these objects might be things like wooden spoons, a cutting board or perhaps a decoration made of wood. If your stove and refrigerator are side by side, you may have counter space between them where you can introduce the wood element. If your sink is directly across from your stove you can use Earth energy as Earth dams up Water and exhausts Fire. Perhaps a square, yellow throw rug would be practical.

When you make the effort to balance and harmonize the energy in your kitchen, the energy in the house will flow more smoothly, and set the stage for a more successful showing.

EVALUATING THE BEDROOMS

When a client is looking at the bedrooms of the house, they should get a feeling of rest and tranquility. If the bedroom is unfortunately placed – in the front of the house, or too close to the kitchen for example– you should takes extra steps before a showing to minimize this challenge. If there is more than one entrance to the room, see if you can close off the one that opens into the busier area. If there are windows overlooking the street or driveway, close the curtains or blinds when possible. Ideally there would be some protective foliage outside the window.

When showing the house, keep shades and blinds at least partially drawn unless you have a spectacular view to show off. A somewhat darkened effect helps set the mood. Of course you don't want anybody stumbling around in the dark, but it is difficult to feel like this is a place where you will get a good night's sleep if you are viewing it in the blazing sunlight.

Although some clients are impressed with a lot of floor space in a bedroom, this is a room that actually works better with less space. Of course there should be room for a bed as well as the night stands, dressers, etc. that are part of any bedroom décor. And ideally there will be more than one possible location for the bed so that the client can choose the location most compatible with their needs and desires. However, when a bedroom has significantly more floor space than is necessary, there is a tendency to use that space to include activities that do not belong in the bedroom. I'm talking about exercise equipment, computer or stereo setups or even laundry/ironing equipment. If you have anything of this nature in the bedroom, do your best to get it moved out prior to a showing. Bedrooms should only be used for sleeping and sex.

Excessive use of mirrors and green plants in the bedroom will also disturb the tranquility. Remember these are objects we use to raise the Chi in a room, and this is a room where we want the energy to drop. Have no more than one mirror in a bedroom, and it should be positioned where you cannot see it from the bed. Round or oval frames on the mirror are preferable to square or rectangular frames. If you do have plants in the bedroom, one large plant is better than several small ones. And no dried flowers ever, dried flowers are dead energy.

This is also the room that is most likely to hold personal photographs and mementos which could make your buyer feel as though they are intruding on somebody else's space. You should make an effort to pack these safely away until the contract is signed. The bedroom is the most intimate room of a house, so be sure there is nothing to prevent your buyer from imagining themselves in this one.

EVALUATING THE BATHROOMS

Because of the inherent nature of a bathroom, you are always going to find a vast amount of Water energy there. Water energy is extremely Yin, and an excess amount can make you tired and lethargic. To counteract this excess Water energy, you should add Wood and Earth element into the area. Wood energy will exhaust Water and Earth dams up or absorbs Water. Plants are a great addition to the bathroom from a Feng Shui viewpoint and lift the Chi as well. Materials and colors of the Earth element work very well also. An easy remedy when you are selling a house would be to use towels in a color representing the earth element; shades of tan or yellow are neutral enough to appeal to buyers of either sex. The wood element could be introduced with clever use of appropriate artwork or decorative objects as well as live plants.

Adding or enhancing mirrors will also lift the Chi. If you are selling a house with a plain expanse of mirror over the sink, frame it with a simple wooden molding to make it look more elegant while adding Wood energy. Mirrors are not only an easy way to attract Chi into the bathroom, but a practical addition to the bathroom as well. Just make certain that you do not have two mirrors placed where they will reflect one another. This creates chaotic Chi and could make the most decisive client start to feel confused and ambivalent about the house they are viewing.

To minimize any energy draining effect from the bathroom to the rest of the home, you should keep the door to this room at least partially closed while showing the house. For the same reason you should always close the lid to the toilet, you certainly don't want it draining the energy needed to close a sale. When you make the effort to balance and harmonize the energy in your bathroom, the energy in the house will flow more smoothly, and set the stage for a more successful showing.

FENG SHUI TIPS AND TRICKS TO ATTRACT A SALE:

- Activate the energy in the Wealth corner (SE) by adding movement, light and sound
- Activate the Helpful People corner with movement, light and sound
- Try to place your for sale sign in the northwest corner of the property if possible. A banner type sign that has some movement works well
- At the end of cul-de-sac, energy can stagnate. To counteract this, hang a wind chime or whirl-a-gig, to keep the energy moving
- Paint the door a different color from anything else
- Enter through the front door when showing a home
- Put 3 lucky coins under the welcome mat
- Close the door to any bathroom that is visible as you walk in
- Place a Jade plant near the front door
- Plant bushes or flowers around a utility box in the yard to deflect attention from it and soften the effect
- Trim any trees or bushes blocking the doors or windows

CHALLENGING FENG SHUI ASPECTS
THE FOLLOWING CHALLENGES ARE VIRTUALLY IMPOSSIBLE TO CHANGE:

- A property where the front door is below street level
- A property where owners (and neighbors) can't get vegetation to thrive
- A front door that opens directly onto a staircase
- Heavy power lines overhead or major power plants nearby
- Close proximity to a cemetery, hospital or meat packing plant
- The ground is composed of wet or sandy soil
- The surrounding ground is higher than the building site
- The property is at the end of a T-junction
- A tree, utility pole or a transmission tower is located directly in front of the door

Note to buyers; if you spot these deficiencies in a property you are considering, you will be best off to walk away no matter what a bargain it appears to be. Although the negative influences of the problems listed above can be mitigated, they can never be complete removed. You will not thrive in a house like this and will have a difficult time when you try to resell it.

Note to Real Estate Professionals: there are certain aspects that should always be avoided from a Feng Shui perspective. If the listing you are considering has several of these characteristics, you will be better off turning it down. When you do not have this option, conserve your energy in showing this particular listing and protect your credibility with potential buyers by not showing it to them until you have exhausted every other possibility of making a sale to this particular client. If you do manage to sell a property with deficiencies like the ones listed above, it will probably not lead to repeat business or glowing referrals.

PREPARING FOR AN OPEN HOUSE

When you use an open house type event to attract buyers you need to know how to make potential buyers feel at home in your house. Realtors are quite aware of how having the seller around during the showing will put a damper on a buyer's enthusiasm. What they might not be aware of is how having too much of the current owners presence around in the form of ambient energy will also cool off a buyer. It inhibits potential buyers and makes it difficult for them picture the property as be their own home. And this shift is necessary if you want to get to the point of signing a contract.

As difficult as it is to do while you are still living in the house, (and occupied houses do sell better than empty ones) you have to counter balance your personal energy in the house and make it feel more like a model home. You have already put your stamp on the house through your choice of paint colors, landscaping and décor, now you need to make it as impersonal as you possibly can while still keeping it warm and inviting.

Removing (storing, selling or giving away) anything that you will not be taking with you to your new home will not only remove predecessor energy, but it will also give you a head start on packing and moving. Be sure to keep the main items required to make it look like a home; such as beds, a sofa and dining room table; until you have a signed contract. You may think these large items the make big difference, but it is all the small stuff that creates the most interference. Don't say that you don't have time to sort clothes for the thrift shop while you are busy moving; you are going to make up all that time when you actually pack out for the final move with the additional bonus of not paying to move them, unpack them, and then finding a place to donate them. When you are done sorting the clothes you are ready to part with, separate all of the off-season clothing you won't need for the time being. You may even want to rent a storage unit to hold these until the moving van arrives. When you show your house now, all of your closets and shelves will look much more spacious. When you are done with the clothes, start on the books, papers, children's toys and even kitchen equipment. If a closet is full the potential buyer will think the house does not have enough closets.

Next, go through the house and pack away all of your family photos and at least half of the knick-knacks. If you have any wall décor with writing on it, pack it away as well. You may think that everyone would appreciate stick on letters that read "Live, Laugh, Love" or "Kiss the Cook", but nobody likes to be told what to think or how to live. Writing or lettering is also distracting and you do want anything to distract the buyers from the process of house hunting. Sometimes after you remove the excess items from your house you may notice scuff marks or smudges on the newly exposed walls. Now is the time to scrub, patch, paint or whatever is necessary to remedy the problem. And don't neglect to also clear your lawn of gnomes, sundials and anything your dog may have left behind. Have the flower beds weeded and watered.

Now that your house cleared and cleaned, and you've made any repairs that became obvious in the process, it is time to set the stage for your open house. Use what you have learned about Feng Shui to attract attention to the best features and deflect it from the areas that are less than perfect. And during the actual showing, make sure there are no intangible distractions as well; no Super Bowl on the big screen and no cooking odors from the kitchen. You may even need to open a few windows if you used cleaning agents with a strong odor or if you have just painted.

The next step is to get to know your home a little better by looking at it through the impersonal eyes of potential buyers. As we do this, you will be using the Feng Shui principles of balance and harmony.

ASSESSING A HOME

USE THE 5 ELEMENT SYSTEM TO ENERGY TYPE A HOUSE

To determine whether a property you are selling is predominately Yin or Predominantly Yang, simply review the characteristics of those two polarities, and determine which you find more of in this particular listing. Yin is low, dark, curving, quiet and spacious while Yang energy is high, bright, straight, loud and crowded. Look at the setting of the home as well as the architectural and decorating style.

Is the property situated on a busy throughway; or at the end of a quiet cul-de-sac?

Is the house located on a corner; or in the middle of the block?

Are the angles of the roof and exterior additions sharp or rounded?

What are the primary colors of the exterior and interior?

How much sun does the house receive; both interior and exterior?

How close together are the homes in this neighborhood? How large are the lots?

The first option in the questions above indicates a house that has mainly Yang energy and the second option describes a house that is predominantly Yin. Homes that are close together are more Yang and large lots give off Yin energy. If your answers to most questions include equal parts of Yin and Yang answers, it is a more balanced energetic type. Either a mainly

Yin or predominantly Yang house will appeal more to certain buyers, but to broaden the appeal to all buyers, you may want to make some adjustments to make it more balanced. It is impossible to move the house from the corner to the middle of the block, but you can offset this Yang energy by introducing more Yin energy in areas where you do have options. Once you have a feeling for whether the house is basically Yin or Yang, you can fine tune your assessment by reviewing characteristics of the five element types. Again, we are looking at the interior, the exterior and the surrounding neighborhood.

ELEMENT TYPES AND BUILDING CHARACTERISTICS

The following descriptions are stereotypes that describe a home with a higher than average number of features that fall into a single energy category. This is for purposes of illustration only, in your daily work you are going encounter homes that are a blending of all the energy types and it will be up to you determine which type, or types, are dominant.

THE FIRE HOUSE

A house with lots of Fire energy is one that faces south and has a prominent entrance. There is most likely to be a front porch, columns, pillars or some other architectural feature that emphasizes the entrance to the home. The house may have double doors, or a front door that is very elaborate in design or decoration.

The exterior color palette could either be in the red family or other bright color. The roof may be pointed or sharply angled, and the house has more than one level. This house is likely to be on a smaller lot, situated close to both the street and the neighboring houses, and quite likely on a corner. There would be more of the yard in front of the house than in back. The street in front of the house is most likely one of the main thoroughfares for this area.

THE EARTH HOUSE

A house with lots of Earth energy is often made of stone or brick or it has a porch or fence made of these materials. It is most likely a single story home with a very gentle pitch to the roof. The shape is either square or rectangular with few if any exterior additions to alter this shape. It can be found on a very level lot with the house situated close to the center of the property.

The exterior color palette may either be yellow, brown or other earth tones. The landscaping is well established and you are quite likely to find a vegetable garden in the back yard. The surrounding neighborhood is made up of very similar houses, and it is located conveniently near shopping facilities.

THE METAL HOUSE

A house with lots of Metal energy is often somewhat of a landmark within its neighborhood. It may stand out in some physical way, or it may be known for an experimental design involving energy efficiency. The house itself, or some of the architectural detailing, will emphasize curves and round ornaments. There may be metal itself in the exterior building materials, or metal may be evident in doors, lawn furniture or out-buildings.

The most common color for a Metal energy house is white, with trim in a neutral color or pastel. The house itself may face west or northwest, with landscaping that includes deciduous trees. The floor plan is a little unusual, but extremely efficient and it is likely to have incorporated the latest developments in electrical conveniences. These homes are often found in newer subdivisions or outlying areas.

THE WATER HOUSE

It will often look as though a house with lots of Water energy has evolved over the years into an irregular sprawl that all but hides the original shape of the building. You are likely to find many additions like porches, decks, sunrooms or breezeways that were not part of the original plan. The house may be located near water, or have a drainage ditch or creek nearby. Ponds, fountains or birdbaths are often found in the yard.

The landscaping is likely to be as "native" as the local zoning boards will allow with an emphasis on wild flowers rather than anything that resembles a formal garden. Many of these homes are one-of-a kind and the previous tenants expressed their eccentricities in both the exterior and interior design. The exterior color will come from a dark color palette, and the yard is most likely fenced completely.

THE WOOD HOUSE

A Wood house is probably made out of just that, wood. Shake roofs are also common, and it is often taller than it is wide. You are likely to find that a potting shed, woodworking shop or wooden decks are part of the package. The yard is completely landscaped, well-tended and usually includes several mature trees and well-established perennials.

The kitchen tends to dominate the interior, and single-purpose rooms are the rule. This is usually a very practical house both in terms of design and materials used and most will have room for future expansion. Attics and basements are probably finished off, and the attached garage may have been converted into a room for some other use. These houses are usually found in neighborhoods filled with growing families and the back yard is usually fenced.

ASSESSING A CLIENT
USE THE 5 ELEMENT SYSTEM TO ENERGY TYPE BUYERS

Now that you know how to determine the energy type of a property, the next step is to perform a similar assessment on your clients. Then you will be able to match clients to the type of house that will make them feel like they are "in their element" and customize your sales approach to appeal to their inner nature. When selling a house to a client with Fire energy – you will want to emphasize the parts of the house that will feed this energy. When selling the same house to a Water type person, you should place your emphasis elsewhere.

ELEMENT TYPES AND INDIVIDUALS

The basic types of elements are the same, but the application to a living, changing, active human being requires a slightly different approach. We are all born with a basic elemental nature – just as we are each born with an astrological sun sign – but this nature is altered by space and time. The way we express our nature as children, will change and mature as we get older. We also alter our way of being (another way of saying our elemental nature) according to the situation we find ourselves in.

Human beings are much more complex than houses or decorating items, and you should not be surprised to learn that we all actually have three layers of elements to our nature. One of these layers, your principle nature, represents your core identity (this would be similar to your sun sign in Western astrology). A second, equally important layer is your energetic nature (akin to your moon sign) which is the elemental nature that you will revert to under pressure. The third layer (comparable to your rising sign in Western astrology) is your character nature and reveals your style of operating. An in-depth analysis of element types on all three levels is beyond the scope of this book; however I have mentioned them here to explain why a person will not always appear to act in accordance with their basic elemental nature. For our purposes, we will be working only with the principle nature, or primary energy type, of potential buyers.

DETERMINING THE ELEMENT TYPE OF A CLIENT

You *could* ask for a client's birth information and have a Feng Shui Astrology chart drawn up, but this is not very practical. As you gain experience working with Feng Shui, you will begin to sense the energy type that your client is exhibiting, but until you reach that stage, here is an easy method to gain some insight. Chinese doctors (who treat their patients according to energy type) will often use the clues offered by a person's hands to determine their basic element type. Since the traditional handshake gives you the perfect opportunity to look at a client's hands, this is a method that you can also use. Following is a list of some of the signs to looking for.

HAND SHAPES AND ELEMENT TYPES

FIRE

Long hand, longer fingers
Bent pinky finger
Convex, oval nails
Gestures a lot – female will often wear bright nail polish

EARTH

Short hand with square palm and thick base
Sausage fingers, flat-rectangular nails
Often holding food

METAL

Long hand, longer palm
Double jointed or crooked fingers
Rectangular nails with vertical lines
Prone to making elegant gestures and to wearing rings

WATER

Short fleshy hand
Loose skin on top of hand or at knuckles
Nails short and thin, they may turn under from weakness
Dark cuticle area

WOOD

Evenly proportioned hand
Several lines both on palm and fingers
Fragile nails with horizontal grooves
Tendency to bite nails when nervous or emotional

THE POWERS OF OBSERVATION

The biggest drawback to hand shape analysis is the situation you are in when you meet a client. Changing residence is stressful under any circumstance, and much of the time the move has been precipitated by another form of stress such as a marriage, a divorce or a job change. Because of this your client will be operating on the energy level where they feel most comfortable – that second layer, the one they revert to under pressure.

A good part of the time your most valuable tool in determining the element type of a client will simply be to observe how they interact with you and with other people. Once you get comfortable using your intuition on this, your grounding in the basic concepts of energy types will be all you need to come to a quick and accurate assessment.

The following list will provide a quick reference to the characteristic traits of a person operating under each of the energy types. The list also has some suggestions as to which areas of the house will hold the most interest for them (and perhaps make or break the sale) showing you where to focus your selling efforts.

An additional point you need to consider is that in most cases you are directing your sales approach to two different people – often a husband and wife. In this case what you should do is accommodate the desires of the man (or the breadwinner) when it comes to the public rooms, and to the desires of the woman (or supportive partner) when it comes the private rooms.

FIRE PERSON

Characteristics: outgoing, impatient, impulsive, dynamic, future oriented
Areas of Interest: Kitchen, Living Room, Porch or Patio
Sales emphasis: Curb appeal, front entrance, large windows, fireplace, impressive living room

EARTH PERSON

Characteristics: Loyal, attentive, thorough, stubborn, and sometimes needy
Areas of Interest: Kitchen, dining room, and workroom
Sales emphasis: Kitchen and dining room, garden and workrooms

METAL PERSON

Characteristics: Perfectionist, controlled, organized, idealistic, and authoritative
Areas of Interest: A library, study or home office
Sales emphasis: Home office, places for home theater or stereo systems

WATER PERSON

Characteristics: Resourceful, independent, imaginative, reflective and quiet
Areas of Interest: Bath, study, or music room – places offering Privacy and solitude
Sales emphasis: Sound-proofing, privacy features, and bathrooms

WOOD PERSON

Characteristics: Practical, open, motivated, competitive, restless
Areas of Interest: A place for books, music, artwork, a place to study, concentrate and create
Sales emphasis: Woodworking shop, gardening areas, study or office

Armed with this information, you can direct your sales efforts to emphasize the areas of interest to the buyer you are working with. By applying the principles of Feng Shui when selling a home you can:

- *Increase the perceived value of a property*
- *Present any listing in the most favorable light*
- *Match a property you list to the most receptive client*

You may be surprised to find this information often can also be of use in your personal and professional life as well as home selling.

A NOTE TO REAL ESTATE PROFESSIONALS

If you have read from the beginning, you now have the foundation in Feng Shui principles that will allow you to offer your clients so much more than the competition. By using your knowledge of Feng Shui to offer a customized approach that addresses the buyers' need for a home that provides more than just shelter, you have positioned yourself on the cutting edge of today's market.

When you look at a potential listing you will now be able to sense not only how a house will *look* to a buyer, but more importantly, how it will *feel* to a buyer. When you can get your client to feel at home in a house they are viewing, it just a few short steps to escrow.

Good Feng Shui is simply abundant Chi, a balance of Yin and Yang and a harmonious link between elements. Well balanced Chi leads to a sense of prosperity and well-being which is exactly the frame of mind that turns lookers into buyers.

Unbalanced Chi creates patterns of conflict – conflict between a husband and wife which means no offer on the house – or conflict between the buyer and seller when it comes to price and terms; again no sale. By using the techniques you have learned to balance Chi and remove those patterns of conflict, you can replace conflict with harmony and benefit from a fast sale. When Chi is in balance, things will flow smoothly and comfortably; easily and effortlessly. Not only does this mean more sales for you, but it means deeper satisfaction for your clients which will in turn bring more referrals and repeat business.

CHECK LIST FOR BUYING OR SELLING A HOME

The check list that follows will come in handy whether you are preparing your own home to put it on the market or you are looking for a new home to buy. As a seller, you can see at a glance where you need to concentrate your efforts; as a buyer you will be able to determine if the positive aspects out-weigh the negative issues. Some aspects will be impossible to change, and others may not be worth the effort to change but seeing them all in one place will make it easier for you to make a decision.

FENG SHUI CHECKLIST – ENTRANCE

Yes answers to questions in this section indicate a positive Feng Shui design and can offset any challenging aspects.

- Is the pathway from the curb slightly curved?
- Can the house numbers be read easily; day and night?
- Are all steps and handrails in good condition?
- Is there an area in front protected from the weather? (A porch for example)
- Does all of the front door hardware work smoothly?
- Is the door itself attractive and well maintained?
- Does the surrounding vegetation complement the entrance?
- Is the entrance well lighted?

Yes answers to questions in this section indicate a challenging Feng Shui design. Correct as much as you can and deflect attention from what you can't change.

- Do you see any clutter on the porch or near the door?
- Are there any burned out bulbs in the exterior lighting?

- Have any shrubs or bushes over-grown the walkway or entrance?
- Are the house numbers too small, invisible at night or in need of repair?
- Are there any dead or dying plants on the porch or entry?
- Are there any empty planters in view?
- Are any windows cracked or dirty?
- Is the doorbell in need of repair?
- Does the door stick or creak when opened?

FENG SHUI CHECKLIST – FOYER

Yes answers to questions in this section indicate a positive Feng Shui design and can offset any challenging aspects.

- Is the area well illuminated?
- Is there a place to put down packages within 10 steps of the door?
- Does the front door open completely and easily?
- Are there adequate accommodations for hats, coats and boots?
- Is there a mirror for arriving guests or departing occupants?
- Is there a chair or bench to sit on while removing footwear?
- Is flooring designed for indoor/outdoor traffic?
- Does a plant or floral touch bring the outdoors in?
- Is the area decorated to complement the home?

Yes answers to questions in this section indicate a challenging Feng Shui design. Correct as much as you can and deflect attention from what you can't change.

- Is the back wall less than 6 feet from the front door?
- Does the main entrance enter directly into a room with no buffer zone?

- Can a bathroom or kitchen be seen from the foyer?
- Is there anything stored behind the door?
- Are there any family photographs or memorabilia on display?
- Is there anything blocking your movement into the house itself?
- Are there any burned out or flickering light bulbs?
- Have the table tops become a catch-all for clutter?

FENG SHUI CHECKLIST – LIVING ROOM

Yes answers to questions in this section indicate a positive Feng Shui design and can offset any challenging aspects.

- Is the room located near the front of the house?
- Are there large windows with a commanding view?
- Is there a foyer or entry hall as a buffer zone from the door?
- Do the windows have a pleasant view?
- Are there adequate storage options for things kept in this room?
- Are the walls and floor coverings clean and fresh?
- Are sofas and chairs arranged into conversation areas?

Yes answers to questions in this section indicate a challenging Feng Shui design. Correct as much as you can and deflect attention from what you can't change.

- Has the room become a catch-all for clutter?
- Do you walk directly in from the front door?
- Are there private rooms (Bedroom or bath) opening directly into the living room?
- Is overhead lighting the only choice available?
- Is the room located behind the centerline of the house?
- Are there more than three (3) ways of entering the room?

FENG SHUI CHECKLIST – DINING ROOM

Yes answers to questions in this section indicate a positive Feng Shui design and can offset any challenging aspects.

- Does the dining room or eating area have windows to the outdoors?
- Is there plenty of room to get in and out of the chairs around the table?
- Does the room have adequate overhead lighting?
- Is the kitchen conveniently located?
- Can guests enter the dining room without going through private rooms?
- Are the wall and floor coverings appropriate to the way the room is used?
- Do green plants bring the room to life?
- Is there a way to enjoy music while dining?
- Are the walls and floors clean and fresh?

Yes answers to questions in this section indicate a challenging Feng Shui design. Correct as much as you can and deflect attention from what you can't change.

- Is the dining room seldom used in this home?
- Is the room located in an energetic "dead-end"?
- Does a bathroom door open directly into the dining room?
- Is the room accessible only by going through the kitchen?
- Has the room become a catch-all for clutter?
- Is the room designed with few or no windows?
- Is the view from the windows less than desirable?
- Has the carpet or other floor covering become stained with use?
- Is the furniture too crowded for ease of movement at the table?

FENG SHUI CHECKLIST – THE KITCHEN

Yes answers to questions in this section indicate a positive Feng Shui design and can offset any challenging aspects.

- Is the room located away from the front door?
- Can the cook see the entrance to the room while working?
- Does the room have one or more windows?
- Do the fire element appliances and the water element features have adequate separation?
- Is the room well ventilated, preferably with outside air?
- Is the room well lighted?
- Are all appliances and plumbing in good working order?
- Is the entire room clean and fresh?
- Is there a back door here or other outside entrance?

Yes answers to questions in this section indicate a challenging Feng Shui design. Correct as much as you can and deflect attention from what you can't change.

- Is the stove located immediately next to the refrigerator and/or sink?
- Is the room facing a southerly direction?
- Are there any leaks or drips in the sink or appliances?
- Do the drains or taps show signs of corrosion?
- Is there any evidence of mold or mildew?
- Are floor coverings and surfaces designed to withstand heat and moisture?
- Is the oven or any burner malfunctioning?
- Are there any musty smells or lingering odors of stale food?
-

FENG SHUI CHECKLIST – BEDROOMS

Yes answers to questions in this section indicate a positive Feng Shui design and can offset any challenging aspects.

- Is the room located away from the front door?
- Is there a choice of bed placement?
- Does the closet door completely cover the opening?
- Will the main door close off the room completely?
- Does the door have a functional lock?
- Does the room have one or more outside windows?
- Does any attached bathroom have a separate entrance?
- Do the windows have a pleasant view?
- Are the walls and floor coverings clean and fresh?

Yes answers to questions in this section indicate a challenging Feng Shui design. Correct as much as you can and deflect attention from what you can't change.

- Is the room located near the front of the house?
- Are there too many mirrors or plants in the bedroom?
- Is overhead lighting the only choice available?
- Can you see the toilet from the bed?
- Are there power lines or utilities located directly outside the window?
- Are the windows so large they make the occupants feel exposed?
- Are street noises or driveway activity heard through the windows?
- Does the room still contain personal photographs or mementos?
- Is there any inappropriate equipment in the room? (Ironing board, exercise equipment, etc.)

FENG SHUI CHECKLIST – BATHROOMS

Yes answers to questions in this section indicate a positive Feng Shui design and can offset any challenging aspects.

- Is this room located away from the front door?
- Does the door have a secure lock that works easily?
- Is the room well ventilated with outside air?
- Is the toilet out of your direct line of sight as you open the door?
- Are there live plants in the room providing Wood energy?
- Does the owner keep the lid down and the door closed when not in use?
- Are the floor and wall coverings designed to withstand moisture?
- Is it adequately lighted for the normal use of the room?
- Is the design of the room one that is easy to keep clean?

Yes answers to questions in this section indicate a challenging Feng Shui design. Correct as much as you can and deflect attention from what you can't change.

- Is the room located near the front of the house?
- Is the room directly adjacent to the kitchen?
- Is the bathroom located in a power corner of the house?
- Is the lighting dim, or malfunctioning?
- Are there any musty or moldy smells in the bathroom?
- Are there any signs of leaks around the tub, sink or toilet?
- Are any of the fixtures stained or chipped?
- Is the door lock missing or hard to operate?
- Is there intimate clutter on shelves and surfaces?

Whether you are buying or selling, there is no formula for determining the number of yes answers that make a property desirable from a Feng Shui standpoint Only *you* will know which challenges are possible to eliminate based on your skills and budget.

USING FENG SHUI TO REMOVE CHALLENGES

As you read the list of Feng Shui challenges, you probably noticed that some of them would be very easy to fix, and that is where Feng Shui cures and remedies come into play. When we think of applying Feng Shui remedies, the first thing we usually think of is increasing the Chi in a particular area. Adding light, sound or living things to an environment are the most effective ways to increase the amount of energy in an area or to enhance the quality of that energy.

Sometimes these remedies are second nature to us. Have you ever walked into a gloomy room and instinctively gone to open the drapes or turn on the stereo? You may not have thought of yourself as applying Feng Shui remedies, but that was exactly what you were doing. After reading the next chapter, you will be able to make adjustments to the energy of a space even when the problem and the cure are not as obvious.

When was the last time you shopped in a department store that didn't have piped in music? Do you make use of this sound cure when you show a house? And don't forget the power of your own voice as you are showing a home, the right tone can help create the energy you need to make a sale.

But what about a situation where the obvious or desired remedies are not practical? This is where your knowledge of Feng Shui will enable you to achieve the same results with whatever you have available. By understanding the principles behind the remedies you will be in a position to make substitutions that will fit whatever time or budget constraints you might be faced with. Begin with the basic cures of light, sound and light force as outlined below, and refer to the Cures and Remedies chapter if you want more suggestions.

LIGHT

Mirrors have been called the "aspirin of Feng Shui", but they are not the only reflective surface that can raise the energy in your home. Shiny brass fixtures or silvery ornaments will also produce this effect. When working with light you can increase the amount of natural light, without actually adding a window, simply by changing the type of window covering you use or how you use the window coverings you have. For example, leaving the blinds open to a greater degree will increase the amount of light in a space. Artificial lighting is even easier to manipulate than natural light. You have the option of adding more lamps, increasing the wattage in existing light fixtures (but never above the manufacturer's recommendations) or repositioning what you currently have. You can also use candles, either literally or symbolically. Even when you do not light them, candles symbolize Fire energy and will raise the Chi simply through their presence and your intentions. Adding light raises the energy in a room and reducing the light will lower it.

SOUND

We have all experienced the change when lively music is added to a dull party or a grueling exercise class. It immediately raises the level of energy in that space, and all other energies, including human energy, will rise up to match it. When you want to remove stagnant energy or raise the vibrational level of existing energy, sound is often the fastest and most effective tool at your disposal. If you are in a situation where you can't apply the obvious sound cures, try hanging a wind chime where you can activate it when you enter a low energy room; ring the doorbell before you enter your house (especially if it is unoccupied) and never forget the power of your own voice.

LIFE FORCE

When working in your own home, you will have an option that will not be practical in most selling situations; and that is the addition of actual life force. Although pets are a wonderful source of life force, it is not a good idea to have a dog or cat in residence while you are showing a house. Green plants are a source of life force that will work better for a home selling situation. And of course there will always be the energy that you, yourself, carry. Do not underrate the power of something as simple as chatting brightly while you accompany a client through a gloomy basement area. Encourage the buyers to talk too; the livelier the conversation is, the higher the energy field it creates will be.

SLOWING DOWN RUSHING CHI

There may be times when the energy in a home is moving too fast and you want to slow it down. If this happens when showing a house and you may find your clients rushing out before they have a chance to fall in love the house you are showing them. If you were to bring a client into a house and hear them say "I could stay here forever!" you know it is just a few short steps to escrow. But if the client can't wait to get out of there – it is highly unlikely that there will be a sale forthcoming.

If the energy patterns of a house or a room are moving too fast, your client is going to feel rushed and in a hurry as well. This overly fast movement of Chi can come from one of several sources. One common situation is where the back door is in a direct line with the front door. This "corridor of misfortune" can also be created by having a patio window or other large expanse of glass in this position rather than a back door. Long, straight hallways will also rush the energy along as will any sharp angles or edges.

When you want to change the energy in a room, think back to what you learned about the 5 Elements in the first section. Fire, Metal and Wood are Yang elements that can increase the level of energy in a room. Earth and Water are Yin elements that can lower the level of energy when a more serene atmosphere is desired. Remember; Yang is fast and Yin is slow. Introduce Yang elements to raise energy levels and Yin elements to lower it. Once you have created the right balance of Yin and Yang to suit the intended purpose of an area, Element remedies can be introduced through colors, shapes, materials or objects in the desired category to achieve harmony.

To add Fire energy use leather or fur objects; triangular or radiant shapes and colors from the red family. To increase Wood energy, use plants or wooden objects; tall, rectangular shapes and shades of green. For more Earth energy use clay, tiles, or bricks; square, flat shapes and colors ranging from yellow to brown. When you want to add Metal energy, install clocks or electronics; round and oval shapes; or objects that are white or metallic. If it's more Water energy you want, you can use an actual water feature like a fountain or an aquarium, or use wavy, irregular shapes and the color black (or very deep shades of blue, green or purple). The following list is divided by categories to make it easier to find what kind of energy is already in the space you are working with and give you some ideas about what you can add to, or remove from, this area to balance the energy harmoniously.

COLORS

- All Shades of Green (Wood energy)
- Yellow, Brown, Neutral Tones (Earth energy)
- White, Gold, Silver (Metal energy)
- Red, Pink, Burgundy, Orange (Fire energy)
- Black, Dark Blue, Dark Purple (Water energy)

SHAPES

- Tall Verticals (Wood energy)
- Flat Squares (Earth energy)
- Circles, Ovals (Metal energy)
- Triangles, Obelisks (Fire energy)
- Wavy, Irregular Shapes (Water energy)

MATERIALS

- Plants, Flowers, Bamboo (Wood energy)
- Tile, Stone, Pottery (Earth energy)
- Gold, Silver, Copper (Metal energy)
- Leather, Bone, Fur (Fire energy)
- Glass, Mirrors, Non-metallic reflective surfaces (Water energy)

OBJECTS

- Potted Plants, Flower Arrangements (Wood energy)
- Statuary, Crockery, Decorative Rocks (Earth energy)
- Clocks, Coins, Electronic Equipment (Metal energy)
- Lights, Candles, Radiant Displays (Fire energy)
- Fountains, Aquariums (Water energy)

FENG SHUI CURES AND REMEDIES

This where most people start getting excited – they want to know where to hang that mirror so they can get married by next year. But if you want Feng Shui to really work, you can't skip the basic steps. They may not be glamorous, but they are more transformational than any Feng Shui remedy you can apply. Traditional Feng Shui cures (also called remedies) can be divided into nine basic categories. Some of these categories encompass remedies that can raise the energy of a space; others will hold the energy and slow down rushing Chi. Cures in all the categories can be used for either purpose, depending on how they are applied. Let's take a look at the nine categories and then discuss how they are used and in what situations they would be most effective.

CATEGORIES OF FENG SHUI CURES

- Light producing or reflecting objects – Mirrors, light, crystals
- Sound producing objects– Wind chimes, bells, music
- Life force – Plants, pets, fish, landscaping
- Weighty and heavy objects – Statues, urns, rocks
- Color enhancements– 5 elements, and Bagua correspondences
- Water Features – Aquariums, birdbaths, fountains
- Energy or Fire producing objects – Electronics, lights and candles
- Ritual objects – Flutes, paintings, chimes, crystals
- Transcendental cures – Intentions, Affirmations

HOW THEY WORK

Whether you call them cures or remedies, they all work in one of three ways: they alter the flow of Chi, or balance the Yin and Yang or they harmonize the link between the elements. This flow, balance and harmony are the three building blocks of Feng Shui that we covered in depth in the first section of this book.

REMEDIES TO ALTER CHI

With Feng Shui you can alter Chi in five ways. You can: attract; raise; lower; disperse or deflect Chi depending on the situation and what you are trying to achieve. Most of this was covered in the earlier section about Chi, but it can be helpful to review these basic adjustments by thinking of them as cures and remedies.

Good Chi begins at the front door. It is affected by the yard or outside of your building as well as the neighborhood you live in. If your home is located on a coast, shoreline or on a busy street; you will have an abundance of Chi in your home as long as you do not have any obstructions in the way. If you live a location like this, you are more likely to be troubled by Chi that moves too quickly and may need to work with ways of deflecting or slowing it down, it rather than attracting it.

If you have an area of your personal or professional life where nothing is happening, this will usually be reflected in the corresponding area of your home as either a lack of Chi or stagnating Chi. For example, if you have been at the same job for a significant period of time and not getting the recognition you deserve in form of a raise or promotion, take a look at the Career Corner of your living space. Make note of how much Chi enters this area. If the north part of your house is a long way from the front door or does not have any windows, you can attract more Chi by using one or more of the nine categories of cures listed earlier in this chapter. If there are no windows in the area, the first cure to try would be a light producing cure; additional lamps for example or perhaps a mirror placed where it will reflect (and thereby increase) the nearest source of natural light. If your Career corner is out of the main path of activity in your home you can add one of the life force cures like a healthy plant which will attract Chi to the area. Depending on your lifestyle and what is in the north part of your home, you could move your stereo equipment here (sound cure) or even set up a sleeping or play area for your pet (life force remedy) to attract Chi.

If there is plenty of Chi entering your Career area, check to see if it is stagnating. This problem is common in alcoves or other areas with no outlet to keep the Chi moving or when the natural outlet is blocked by furniture. Make sure there is a way for the Chi to move on once it has lingered just long enough to nourish the area. On the opposite end of the spectrum, perhaps you have enough Chi entering, but it moves through so quickly that it does not nourish the space with energy. If this is the case you want to slow it down by either blocking the exit; choosing objects that will slow down the Chi (soft surfaces rather than hard), or by adding light, sound, or motion cures to symbolically slow down the Chi by grabbing its attention.

If your job appears to be of the dead-end variety, you will want to raise the Chi in the Career corner and if you experience a lot of conflict in this part of your life, you may want to lower the energy level in this area. Remember, where your attention goes; energy flows. To raise the energy you want to remove anything that brings your attention down. This might be a floor length table covering, trailing vines or even a brightly patterned rug. To raise the energy level you want to eliminate these things and to lower the energy level you would want to add more of these things. Changing the energy level in a room can be as simple as repositioning the artwork you display by raising or lowering it an inch or two. Art is normally hung so that the center of the picture is at eye level. Anything that causes you to raise your eyes will raise the energy level in the room and whatever causes you to lower your eyes, with lower the energy level.

You also want to look at the Feng Shui corner directly across from the area you are working on. In this example we are working on the Career corner in the north, so we need to look at the south which is our Fame corner. What happens in one Feng Shui corner will be reflected in the opposite corner as well. Revisit the Bagua and make note of the relationships it shows. Your Career is reflected in your Fame area and Helpful People is reflected in your Wealth area, etc. This is why you want to follow up the work you have done in the Career area by moving to the Fame area to evaluate the flow, balance and harmony in that area and then apply any remedies indicated.

Remember: Discordant Chi creates patterns of conflict and well balanced Chi leads to a sense of well-being and prosperity.

BALANCING YIN AND YANG

When your environment is in balance, your life will flow comfortably and effortlessly. The obvious question is, "a balance of what?" and the answer to that is: Yin and Yang. Any room with a designated function will work better if the dominant energy in that room supports the intended function, however it must always be a balance. Too many overstuffed, over-draped fixtures in a room will create a room with excessive Yin and make you feel stuffy, sad and lethargic. Too many hard, reflective, surfaces can create an excessively Yang atmosphere that will make you feel jumpy, exposed and vulnerable.

You learned in the first section of this book that you need abundant Yang energy in any area where what you do requires focus, concentration or action. Your home office, art studio or work-out room would fall into this category. Areas like your bedroom, dining room or reading nook need a Yin atmosphere to support the functions for which they are intended. However any area might need to have its energy rebalanced if it is being used for a singular event. For example a quiet living room or family room with Yin energy that promotes relaxation for a quiet evening at home will need an infusion of Yang energy if you plan to use it for a party. Because it is a temporary need, you will make different choices when deciding what kind of remedies to use. If you wanted a permanent remedy you might change the paint color or floor covering to increase the Yang energy, but since this is a temporary use of the room, it will be easier to introduce bright Yang colors through disposable decorations. Sound and light remedies are ideally suited to making temporary adjustments because they can be changed quickly and easily. You can even change the energy during the event itself. In our party example, when it is time to call it a night, you can turn off some lights and change the tempo of the music you're playing.

Never make the mistake of thinking that the carefully balanced Yin and Yang atmosphere you orchestrated when you first designed your space will remain your ideal balance forever. There are changes during the year, for example as winter gives way to summer you no longer light the fireplace on cold evenings, so the focal point of the living room moves from the fireplace to the large, open windows and you will change the furniture placement to reflect that change. People are naturally more active in during the bright days of summer and that also brings more Yang energy into the home which will need to be balanced out. We all do a little re-balancing every single day as the evening changes to night and night gives way to daylight. Without even thinking about why, we turn out the lights, close curtains and blinds and soften or eliminate any unnecessary sounds as we prepare for sleep and reverse the process when we rise to meet the day.

It is important to make a conscious effort to rebalance the energy in your living environment after any major life change. These changes might include death or divorce or other change in family size like a new baby or older children leaving the nest. At times like this we are reminded of what needs to be done because we are often re-purposing rooms and adjusting our daily routines. Now that you are more familiar with Feng Shui principles, you can use that knowledge to rebalance the energy in your home to attract a change that you want to make. If you have reached the stage of like where you would like to find a mate and settle down, your first step should be to create the environment that will support that change. In this example you should concentrate your efforts in the Relationship corner of your house and in the bedroom regardless of the corner where it is located. If a woman would like to find a husband, she should first of all make sure her bed is large enough to accommodate a couple, and then reorganize the closet and dresser to create enough empty space to make room for a second person using the room. To support an equal partnership, arrange equal access to lamps and clocks from either side of the bed. Make sure that the bed is not placed up against a wall – that is an arrangement that only works for a single person and you are sending out the subconscious message that you want to remain that way.

LINKING THE ELEMENTS

The third building block of Feng Shui is a harmonious link between the elements. When you want to improve your success in some area of your life such as academics, relationships or career refer to the Bagua map to determine where that life aspect is anchored energetically in your home. Review the characteristics on correspondences of the elements from the first sections of this book and see which of the elements dominates the area you are working on. For example, if someone were undertaking a rigorous study schedule like pre-med or law school, they would know that they needed to carve out a dedicated study area where they will not be disturbed. But using the principles of Feng Shui, you will have a better idea of which part of the home or what area of that room would be most conducive to studying. You also know that the energy level (Chi) needs to be fairly high and the energy type needs to be predominantly Yang. After applying any remedies needed to adjust these to fit the intended function of the room, it is time to harmonize the elements.

You can review the characteristics of the elements in chapter three at any time to remind yourself of the correspondences that create the most supportive environment. In this example of a study area, we want Metal energy, and you can bring in this energy in with colors (white or silver gray) and shapes (round or oval) as well as actual metal. A file cabinet or bookshelves can be made of metal as easily as out of wood and if given a choice, choose the metal. Electronics and clocks carry Metal energy and are also quite practical for a study area.

A quick look at the cycle charts in third chapter of this book will show us that Fire controls Metal and Water exhausts it while Earth is the element that produces Metal. Now we know that we want to limit the amount of Fire and Water energy in the area and add some Earth energy to bolster the Metal. Take a look around at the furniture and other objects you have in this room as well as the colors and shapes in it. You probably have a good mixture of energy types already in the room, and all you need to do is a little minor tweaking until you feel that you have them in harmony. The final proof of your success will be how well you can study in this room when you are done. If you find yourself daydreaming or becoming lethargic while studying, try replacing some of the soft surfaces with hard ones or add some Fire energy with a red notebook or lampshade. Remember red is a powerful color and a little goes a long way. There is no "cookbook" or "one-size-fits-all" solution to balancing the energy in your space. Just apply the basic principles and then learn to trust your feelings. After a little trial and error you will be adept at optimizing any area for its intended use.

SPACE CLEARING

Step one is to clean your house and remove all your clutter. These are two separate actions; don't confuse clutter with dirt and grime. Clutter is anything in your life that you don't absolutely need or absolutely love. Feng Shui cures will work to some extent without these steps, but to really work some magic, you need to start at the beginning. It's like applying makeup to a face that hasn't been washed, or putting ointment on a wound that hasn't been cleaned; you'll notice some improvement, but nothing like what you would get if you prepared the area first.

Once you have removed the visible obstacles of grime and clutter the next step is to remove the unseen obstacles and limitations that are anchored in your psychic energy field. We do this with what is called a Space Clearing, and this is the secret ingredient that makes some people's Feng Shui efforts so much more successful than others who skip this step.

You know you would think at least twice before buying a home where a murder had taken place – but it doesn't take something that dramatic to leave negative energy in a space. It can be just as important to know if the former occupants suffered bankruptcy or divorce, or a lingering illness.

Just like we carry stress in our bodies as tension, hard luck and misfortune are imprinted in our environment as negative energy. If you have just come out of a relationship that that ended badly, you should at least do a clearing and blessing on your bedroom and in your Relationship corner to increase your chances of attracting a better relationship in the future.

Have you ever walked into a room after an argument and commented that you could "cut the air with a knife?" What you are feeling in a situation like that is negative energy and you need to remove any negative energy that might be lingering in your home if you want to attract health, wealth and happiness.

WHAT IS IT?

Space Clearing is a ceremony or procedure that will remove any negative energy that lingers in a space and might have a harmful effect on the occupants. This negative energy can be created through grief caused by illness, death, violence, misfortune or a lack of love.

Space Clearing is essential if you have moved into a home where the previous occupants suffered divorce, bankruptcy, major illness or violence. If you don't know the fate of the previous occupants, it is a good protective tool. If you have had these or any other misfortunes and are starting over in the same space, house clearing is even more vital because this negative energy is yours and it will affect you even more than negative energy left behind by others.

Space clearing can remove many of the limitations and obstacles you may have in your life now. Clearing your space also gets your home ready for blessing ceremonies or life enrichment rituals.

WHY DO I NEED IT?

You are probably aware of the dramatic changes you can make in your life by removing the physical clutter in your home. Space Clearing has to do with removing the psychic clutter around you. The negative energy that some people called bad vibes back in the 70's can build up in your home in several ways.

The first way is through what we call predecessor energy. This negativity is a result of what went on in the space before it was yours. Perhaps the couple who lived there before you went through bankruptcy proceedings, or maybe they fought a lot and eventually got divorced. In either case the negative energy that was produced by this is still around and because like attracts like it is setting up negative patterns for your own life. If a crime or other tragedy occurred in your space, you will have a lot of predecessor energy to clear. If you think back, you can probably remember a house in your neighborhood or elsewhere that ended up on the market repeatedly because the owners split up. Or maybe you know of a commercial property where one business after the other failed even though the location and everything else seemed right. These situations were quite likely caused by the effects of predecessor energy.

You may have created the negative energy yourself, especially if you are now trying to start over in the same space after enduring some medical, personal or financial catastrophe. There are also many milder forms of negative energy that we all fall victim to. Whenever we bring home anger, coldness, hostility or stress, that energy becomes part of our environment and will linger even after we have forgotten what was bothering us. We hold stress as tension in our bodies, and in our homes we hold stress as negative energy. Unless you clear your space periodically this will build up and form obstacles and limitations in your life that can prevent you from achieving your goals. Space clearing should be done frequently if you have a lifestyle that subjects you to large amounts of stress for which you have no physical outlet.

A third way that negative energy invades our space is environmental Chi. Chi is the universal energy or life force from which we draw our own energy. If the Chi or energy around your home is hostile or chaotic, it can invade your home quickly unless you do something to clear your space. Some conditions that can create bad environmental Chi would be large power lines over your home, a busy street in close proximity, unpleasant neighbors or a nearby factory that produces fumes or noise. And if you live near a funeral home, hospital, packing plant or the like, the negative energies of those places will gradually seep into your own space in spite of all the precautions you take. The solution is simple and effective. You need to perform a basic space clearing ritual on a regular basis. How often will depend on the specifics of your own circumstances, but most people do this at least twice a year at the change of seasons as well as when they are in the circumstances like the following:

WHEN DO I DO IT?

- When you move into a new home or make changes to your existing home
- When you want to change the atmosphere of your home
- When you've had a serious illness or death in the family
- When you want a new job or a promotion
- When you want to attract wealth or a new relationship
- When you want to enhance your health and vitality
- When you are beginning or ending a significant relationship
- When you are preparing for a House Blessing or Feng Shui enhancement
- Whenever you would like to improve the energy in your home and attract new and better things into your life

HOW DO I DO IT?

A thorough housecleaning should be the first step in removing these negative energies. Some of the methods used after a physical cleaning include burning sage, lighting candles, applying essential oils [Aromatherapy], prayer and the use of prayerful sounds like chanting, chimes, bells or drums. The traditional ritual outlined below, will require something to make noise with and a stick of sage. You can substitute clarifying essential oils or even Bach's flower remedies for the sage by diluting them with water and using a spray bottle. If you use the sage; light the smudge stick and blow gently into it to get the smoke started. Wait until the smudge stick begins to smolder and send up gentle wisps of smoke. Use the smoke to symbolically cleanse your cercmonial tools and yourself.

Always consider safety when working with a smudge stick. Light it and carry it over a fireproof/heat resistant container.

It is very hard to tell when the fire is out. You should wrap the stick in several layers of foil and leave it in your sink or tub overnight for complete safety.

To break up the old patterns, and ready the space for new and better opportunities, begin with sound. Sound is a vibration, or form of energy, and it is excellent for breaking up negative energy patterns in your home. You may want to have a special drum, rattle or chime for this ritual, or you can use whatever you happen to have that makes a nice sound. You can simply use your own hands and clear with a clapping sound. Instruments that make a big sound, like drums or large bells, can move the energy quickly and are great for clearing out negative energy. The delicate sounds that come from chimes, small bells, or even singing, are wonderful for introducing fresh, new energy patterns. Below are some suggestions on how to use the various possible instruments, and feel free to use your own idea for a substitute.

BELLS OR CHIMES

Use any pleasant-sounding bell or chime. You can use a large bell or chime to ring loudly when clearing and a smaller one to ring softly when you want to introduce fresh, new energy.

CLAPPING OR CLICK STICKS

Hand clapping is the traditional method used in China. Loud, sharp claps to drive out the old and gentle "applause" to bring in the new. Sticks are similar. If you do not have traditional click sticks, you can substitute any two sticks, or even pencils. Tap these together instead of clapping your hands. The latter is my personal preference because I find it very easy to hear the change in energy vibrations using wooden pencils.

DRUMS

Drums are wonderful if you have one. Their deep sounds clear energy quickly and are very efficient for large spaces. With sticks, drums or rattles, begin with a rhythm that sounds like a heartbeat. Use a faster rhythm when you want to move stagnant energy.

RATTLES

Rattles will clear stale energy very quickly and are probably the fastest way to introduce new energy. Shake vigorously to clear out old energy and then shake gently to fill the space with new, clearer, energy.

To perform this clearing ceremony, begin in your Wealth corner and end in the center of your home. Use the instrument of your choice to sound out the energy in your home. Move in a clockwise direction and make your sound around the perimeter of each room. Open the closet and cupboard doors and let the sound in there too. It helps to begin with a rhythm that sounds like the human heartbeat and vary this according to what you sense as you move through the area. When you encounter a pocket of negative energy, you will notice that the sounds are not as clear. A bell may sound flat, or a rattle may sound muffled. This is your cue to make more noise, increase the level and speed of the sounds you are making to break up the stagnant energy. You will hear when the notes are clear again. After you have made the rounds breaking up the old energies with your loud noise, go around a second time making a softer, sweeter sound, to introduce new energy of a higher vibrational nature. End up in the middle of your living area, this is your center or home base; the spot from which your life flows and circulates.

Now that you have broken up the old patterns, you want to clear out the negative energy you have disrupted. Traditionally you do this by smudging with herbs. Sage is wonderful for this.

You can buy loose sage and light it with charcoal starters, or you can buy a pre-made smudge stick where the sage is bundled into a stick form and wrapped with string. Use a candle to light the sage because matches won't burn long enough. Blow gently into the end of the stick to get the embers smoldering and watch for wisps of smoke to trail out. If your eyes start burning or you start coughing, you're overdoing it. You want the scent of the herbs, not a smoke screen.

Move through the area again using prayer feathers, or your hand, to direct the smoke around the edges of each room. Many people like to stop in the center of each room and send smoke to the four directions as well as Grandfather Sky and Grandmother Earth. Then they will let the smoke drift heavenward for a moment and thank the Great Spirit for the blessings that are sure to come as well as the ones already received.

Open the windows if possible to make it easier for the air to circulate and regenerate. If you are doing this space clearing during the kind of weather that won't permit open windows, finish up by scattering a small amount of rock salt around in each room. The rock salt will absorb any negativity you have stirred up. Let it stand for at least 24 hours before sweeping or vacuuming.

Whenever you combine the powers of thought with the power of your intentions and reinforce it with physical action, you can make dramatic changes in your life through the mind/body/spirit connection.

When you've completed this ritual you will notice that the energy is crisper, colors will look brighter, sounds will be clearer and the air itself will seem more vibrant. This is because you have created the kind of energy patterns that encourage the flow of prosperity, happiness and vibrant good health into your life.

HOME BLESSING CEREMONY

Clearing and blessing your home is best when done when your space is clean and uncluttered, and you have performed a Space Clearing ritual. Here is a traditional ceremony that incorporates what is called the Three Secret Reinforcements which are:

- Physical Action
- The Creative Voice
- Transcendental Intentions

The physical action will be your movements through the house as you light the candles and the transcendental intentions are what you will be establishing a little further on in this section. You will be incorporating the creative voice as you speak them out loud.

For the ceremony that follows, you will need nine candles; one of each color in the Bagua. [Purple, Red, Pink, Green, Yellow, White, Blue, Black and Grey] You can also put colored ribbons, thread, or paper around simple white candles instead to correspond with the Feng Shui colors. Place these candles around your home somewhere in the Feng Sui Corners that they represent.

Safety First *Burning candles should only be used on a protected, heat resistant surface, away from anything flammable and out of the reach of children and pets.*

SETTING YOUR INTENTIONS

Every aspect of your life is anchored energetically in your home. Think about what you would like to create in each of these areas of your life and make some notes if you wish. Some examples are given here to help you get started, but they are only examples. Your intentions must come from your heart.

NORTHWEST
I light this Grey candle in my area of Helpful People in gratitude for the help I have already received and in anticipation of the help I know is yet to come.

WEST
I light this white candle in my Creativity area to stimulate fresh ideas in my artistic projects and new solutions to my personal problems.

CENTER
I light this yellow candle in the center; my area of unity, and I ask for a long and healthy life for all who enter here.

SOUTHWEST
I light this pink candle in my relationship area and I ask for success in attracting and maintaining healthy relationships in my life. I ask for mutually supportive relations with my family and for mutual enhancement in my personal relationships.

Your intentions may be as simple or as elaborate as you wish. Declare the intentions that you have at this moment in your life; your intentions will change as you grow and change; they are not meant to be permanent. Take a few moments first to consider what is working well in your life and what you would like to change. Set your intentions for each of these areas:

Southeast
Color: Purple
Corresponds with: Wealth, Abundance, Fortunate Blessings

South
Color: Red
Corresponds with: Recognition, Fame, and Self-expression

Southwest
Color: Pink
Corresponds with: Love, Marriage, Relationships

East
Color: Green
Corresponds with: Family, Ancestors, Personal Growth

West
Color: White
Corresponds with: Children and Creative Projects

Northeast
Color: Blue
Corresponds with: Knowledge, Studies, Self-realization

North
Color: Black
Corresponds with: Career, Calling, Your Path in Life

Northwest
Color: Grey
Corresponds with: Helpful People, Angels, Connections, Travel and Hobbies

Center
Color: Yellow
Corresponds with: Tai Chi or Unity, Health and Vitality

As you light each candle, you are going to say out loud; "I am lighting this (*name the color*) candle in my (*name the aspect*) area with the intention of: and state your intentions. Hold the intention clearly in your mind for a moment and then extinguish the candle and move on to the next section. Begin with the Wealth Corner in the southeast part of your house and end with the Health corner in the center.

SUMMARY

You should clear and bless your home approximately every six months or whenever you:

- Move into a new home
- Want to change the atmosphere of a place.
- Bring home a new baby
- Have a death in the household
- Begin an important new project
- Want to increase your vitality

It is also helpful to do a clearing and blessing ritual any time the air feels stale in your home, or when you want to clarify or affirm your direction in life. As you begin exploring Feng Shui you will be tempted to focus on a particular aspect of your life that is very important to you right now. That is a good place to start, but never lose sight of the fact that all of these sectors affect one another and none should be neglected entirely.

CONCLUDING THOUGHTS

Before you begin working on cures and remedies, you should clear your space and clarify your intentions. Then start with the three building blocks of flow, balance and harmony to change the energy in your space.

You can't see energy but you can't see electricity or radio waves either. These waves have always existed, but it was the belief of the man who broadcast the program and the belief of the man who set up the receiver that made radio waves real and tangible. You too can pluck anything you want from the universal energy pool with your beliefs and intentions.

Because we are multi-dimensional beings, there are many ways we can get out of balance. When our life is out of balance, we experience discomfort, pain or illness instead of an easy flow. Any broken object symbolizes something that is not working in your life; either fix it or pitch it. When spaces get dirty, energy will slow and stagnate. Trashcans that are not emptied will do the same thing, and energy will even slow down around dirty clothes hampers. Your surroundings influence your mood, your behavior, your work performance and the way you relate to others. This in turn will affect the way others treat you.

Your home reflects how you relate to yourself, your friends, and your family and to society in general. It shows your areas of difficulty, ease and growth. By incorporating the principles of Feng Shui in your home and office you can expect:

- Success in your business endeavors
- Happiness in your personal life
- Inner peace and positive control

One final word about Feng Shui and the Law of Attraction: This law is often misunderstood to mean that you can attract what you want. The law actually states that you will attract what you are. If you want to attract a loving supportive person, you first have to be one. So what are you?

- You are what you do
- You do what you think about
- You think about what you see

You have the power to change your environment, and *it* has the power to change you.

Chi Thought: *Where your attention goes; energy flows.*

Made in the USA
San Bernardino, CA
09 November 2017